Leadership
and
learning
are
indispensable
to each other.

—John F. Kennedy

Contents

Acknowledgments

This book represents quite a journey—one that was very much like a white-water rafting trip, with numerous rapids to navigate. There are many people to acknowledge. First, I thank my parents for instilling in me the value of endurance. No book could be written without it! Next, I thank the numerous "rafting guides" in my life, those leaders who inspired me and taught me invaluable leadership lessons. Collectively they challenged me to live beyond the ordinary. The list of those folks is rather long, but I would like to mention a few in particular.

To Pat Edgerton, who befriended me when I was a young graduate student and is still my friend and mentor. Your commitment to integrity has had a profound influence on my life. Thank you, Tom Bauer, for encouraging me to live "outside of the box" and make a radical difference. To Paul Hawkins, who first introduced me to the idea that leadership and education are all about relationships. Thank you, David and Carol Boyd, for giving me plenty of room to grow personally and professionally. Your leadership demonstrated deep dedication to those who served with you. To Fraser and Puanana Haug, who invited me to join them in the leadership of a multidisciplinary project in Eastern Europe. That experience was the best on-the-field training I have ever received.

To my colleagues at the University of the Nations, who continually inspire me to lead with integrity. Thank you for believing in me and opening unimaginable doors of opportunity for me around the world. It has changed my life. Thank you, Loren and Darlene Cunningham, for obeying God and laying your lives down to see a vision become a reality. Thank you for inviting tens of thousands of others to join you. I am standing on your shoulders.

To the faculty at Trinity International University—Ted Ward, Perry Downs, Linda Cannell, and Duane and Muriel Elmer—who influenced my life and guided me through the PhD program and the research study upon which this book is based. You challenged me to inquire and to write well! Thank you for everything. You have expanded my world.

Profound thanks to Sandi Tompkins, Betty Barnett, and others in the Kona, Hawaii, writers' group. Each of you helped me navigate the rapid of transitioning from purely academic writing to creative narrative. What a wild rapid that was, but what a fun ride! Thank you for introducing me to my agent, Tim Beals, of Credo Communications LLC. Thank you, Tim, for all of your guidance and for connecting me to Authentic Publishing. Thank you, Volney James, Dana Carrington, and the rest of the staff at Authentic, for believing in my book and seeing it through to publication. Many thanks to my editor, Andy Sloan, for your careful and thoughtful work on the manuscript. Your eyes caught a number of things that I never would have seen. Your enthusiasm about this book deeply encouraged me. Thank you, George Verwer and Peter Maiden, for granting me telephone interviews in the midst of your very busy schedules.

Finally, and most importantly, I thank the Triune God, the only perfect leader, the One whom I have followed since I was a little girl. Your leadership is the most amazing of all. I dedicate this book to you.

Foreword

About three months before the manuscript for this book was due, a casual session of Internet surfing yielded a research article that seized my attention. Published in 2007 in the *Psychologist-Manager Journal*, the article presented statistically significant evidence that generational differences do indeed exist related to leadership values and behaviors. My own research, based on in-depth interviews, had suggested similar results, and I had found empirical evidence. This new research, conducted with data from large groups, however, was very affirming. I was ecstatic!

This book was written to help leaders of all types of

organizations. Whether you lead a nonprofit agency, small business, large corporation, law firm, clinic, school, or church—or teach about organizational development in a university—the principles in this book are relevant to you.

As diversity in the workplace increases, with four generations firmly represented, more data is available for consideration. Evidence indicates that there *are* differences in leadership behavior between the generations. And those dissimilarities create turbulence in the workplace like that found in white-water rapids. But there is a way to navigate through them! We're in this boat together, and diversity doesn't have to mean disaster. In fact, appreciating diversity and learning the skills necessary to dialogue with one another can bring the generations together, allowing for tremendous unity and the strength to tackle the white water of leadership succession. Bring on the rapids!

Preface

Raging, white-foamed water surrounded our black rubber craft. The raft seemed like a bathtub toy compared to the expanse of the river. The noise was deafening. My stomach lurched as we sank into another unexpected drop. Menacing boulders poked up through the water. *Why had I selected Class IV and Class V rapids for my first white-water experience?*

My first white-water rafting expedition was with a group on the New River in West Virginia, with rapids that have special names attached to them. Paddling the tranquil water before the first rapid, I found it hard to believe that we would hit rough waters. But the rafting guide's instructions kept pounding in my head: "Don't lose your cookies." She had informed us that we should navigate that rapid *before* lunch! I was nervous. Suddenly the raft several hundred feet ahead of me disappeared. It simply dropped out of sight. All my senses came to attention.

Fear seized me. My stomach churned. I clutched the oar tightly, preparing myself for the precipitous drop just ahead of me. There was no turning back. We had miles to go and numerous rapids to ford before the adventure would end. I wondered if I would survive. Hours later, exhausted from all the adrenalin that had pumped through my body, we arrived at the end of our journey. I had lived to tell the tale. And I even had a photo to prove it!

Similar thoughts, feelings, and reactions emerge when people are faced with transition in an organization, especially when the change involves leadership. And let's face it—in the life of an organization the time to transfer leadership will come if the group hopes to continue. The first question becomes *What will the transition look like?* Is it possible to prepare for transition in ways that allow for tranquil waters or at least smaller rapids? Does transition have to be tumultuous, wrenching, and as terrifying as Class IV and Class V rapids? How can we pull together to make leadership succession work between generations?

In today's workforce no one is exempt from the fact that four generations are currently represented. From the worlds of business and education to nonprofit organizations and churches, a similar scenario exists. One might find in the same company a seventy-year-old working alongside a twenty-two-year-old. Down the hall, a Gen Xer might be consulting with a

Baby Boomer. What are the defining qualities of each of these generations? Many questions come to the surface:

- Are there generational differences in work ethic—and if so, what are they?
- How does each generation relate and respond to authority figures?
- How does each generation perceive women in leadership?
- What are their expectations in the workplace?
- How do they balance the demands of work and home?
- What are their views about money and fiscal responsibility?
- How does each generation view the role of leadership in an organization?

These questions reflect the need to better understand the values and behaviors of each of these four generations. Research indicates that our perception of leadership is linked to the particular generation in which we grew up. Without that knowledge, transitions in leadership can be very messy. Insight and appreciation of generational differences can prepare a workplace for a much smoother changeover.

The Silent Generation consists of those born between 1925 and 1942. They are the children born during the Great Depression and the generation sandwiched between the first and second world wars. Boomers followed the Silent Generation (1943–1960) and were raised in an era of opportunity, progress, and optimism. They also experienced a radically changing society marked by rebellion, shifting social norms, and outward challenges of authority. Growing up in the shadow of the Boomers, Gen Xers were born between 1961 and 1981. They are technologically savvy and were raised in the age of dual-career families. Finally, Millennials, some of the newest members of the workforce, were born between 1982 and twenty years thereafter. A "plugged-in" generation, they have been around technology since birth. The Internet world of blogs, wikis, podcasts, and ever-present e-mail is as natural to them as breathing.

Each of these distinct groups of people see life differently because of the times in which they grew up. Just consider the differences that might exist in financial matters between those who grew up during the Great Depression and those who were raised in the "instant credit, no-payment-until-next year" society. Might there be a clash between Henry, a member of the Silent Generation who sees leadership as the general who goes to the helm, and Jason, an Xer who is distrustful of leaders and prefers collaboration? You can almost feel the white water forming.

How can we navigate the rapids of transition? The answer to that question is the reason for this book. So grab your oar, don't forget your life jacket, and push off into the white water. It is going to be quite a ride!

Author's Note: Although the demographics and labels (Silent, Boomer, Gen X, Millennial) just described pertain specifically to the United States, the concepts are applicable to other cultures and nations. For example, China went through the Cultural Revolution, which began in the mid-1960s and lasted about ten years. That experience marked a generation; you could name that cohort the "Cultural Revolution Generation," or "CR Generation." Many current Chinese government leaders, exhibiting certain leadership values and behaviors, grew up during that time. Empirical studies referenced in this book have confirmed that. Examples related to other nations around the world abound. Consider India during its push for independence, Germany under Nazism, Yugoslavia under Tito, Korea divided into two nations, and Afghanistan under the Taliban. One wonders how the people growing up in these nations and time periods have perceived leadership. More research is needed, but my educated guess is that such historical events have significantly shaped leadership values and behaviors. In addition, globalization cultivates a far-reaching spread of popular culture via music, television, film, MTV, and especially the Internet. Technology has created a virtual world in which young people around the globe may have solidarity with one another; that is, a generational culture. The principles in this book can be applied beyond the borders of the United States.

PROLOGUE

Meet the Rafting Team

Rumbling down the dirt path to the launch site, the aging yellow bus that once served public schools came to a creaking halt. Daniella, the guide, stood stoically on the riverbank to meet the latest group, their company having paid good money for a white-water adventure. Medium height, bronzed from the sun, and rippling muscles, she has encountered all types. Nothing would surprise her.

The bus door opened. Only four brave souls stepped off—a small band of rafters today. They are a departmental task force from Handover Corp.,* a medium-sized company that was

* Handover Corp. and all of its "employees" are fictitious.

founded in the 1950s in the local area. The company rep told her this was a team-building exercise. Daniella, a Swiss-German, sized them up.

Nate, a tall and lean young man in his early twenties, appears to be in his own world. His black special-edition iPod matches his long dark shorts and is blaring tunes into his ears. A plain white tank shirt exposes a solid tan and well-etched muscles. A simple, black, lattice-looking tattoo circles his right bicep. His head is shaved. Nate hung out at Starbucks last night, researching this rafting expedition. The GPS software on his laptop allowed him a virtual tour of the river, with close-ups of each rapid. He Skyped a buddy of his in the Ukraine who had gone white-water rafting a few months ago, and then he eased into a chatroom to get some more input. He can hardly wait to blog the experience. Hired fresh out of college with a degree in computer security, Nate has been with Handover only a year. He blocks the hackers. Nate has no idea how long he will be with Handover. Maybe he will start his own business in a few years.

Brianna, a blond who just turned thirty-two, looks distracted. She barely made it to the bus on time after dropping off her only child, Abby, at preschool. Her husband, Kyle, owns his own business, and they both work hard, juggling the demands of home and work. At least they share the load equally and have some flextime in their schedules. Handover even allows her to work from home one day a week. She designs webpages and has been with the company for five years. Brianna is short and a little thick in the hips. Too much fast food. But her turquoise-blue tank suit with matching sarong covers most of the overindulgence.

She IM'ed a bunch of friends the day before to talk about this trip and was feeling better about it. A team-building experience would look good on her resume. Who knows how long she will be at Handover? Opportunities abound, and experienced webpage designers are in demand.

Brad is in his late forties and wonders if he can actually do this. Although stocky and athletic, he has suffered from carpal tunnel syndrome and a frozen shoulder in the past year. Besides that, his desk is piled with a backlog of work. He really doesn't have time for this. He sincerely hopes that extra compensation is coming his way for his participation and that he will survive it unscathed. Brad designs software and works extra hours, trying hard to please. Handover is going through some transitions, and he wants to avoid any downsizing. He has twenty years with the firm; but software design could be outsourced. He would like to retire early, at age fifty-five, with a solid pension and then explore other options—like the local golf course. He is expecting a sizeable inheritance. At least he *looks* good in his Eddie Bauer rafting outfit and Ray-Ban sunglasses. A Nike baseball cap covers his head.

George, though the oldest member, is spunky. At sixty-eight his wrinkled face reflects his years, but he stands tall and confident. He could stand to lose a few pounds, but they are mostly concentrated in his paunch. A pork-pie hat sits squarely on his balding head. A navy blue T-shirt hangs loosely over his torso, with the white Handover Corp. logo squarely over his chest. He has worked at Handover his entire career and is proud to be part of the organization. He maintains the computer hardware. George wants to keep working as long as he can. Handover hadn't focused much on team building in the past. But times—they are a-changin'. He can adapt. He is a survivor.

"Good morning," Daniella said rather flatly to the foursome. *How many times have I given this spiel?* "Welcome to the Black River Rafting Expedition. Everyone needs a life jacket, oar, and helmet. Please suit up."

As she observed the foursome rummaging through the bin of life jackets and helmets, a question jogged through her mind: *How do these four folks work together in the same department?*

A totally different question ran through the minds of the Handover group: *Can this tough lady get us safely down the river?*

"Where do you want us to sit in the raft?" asked George, his comment dragging her back to the present. "I'd like to sit in the front, if you don't mind," he said.

Brad rolled his eyes and shot a quick glance at Brianna, who mouthed, "What's new?" Nate was just unplugging his iPod.

Daniella rasped, "Just get in. We'll sort it out in a few minutes. I've got the rudder position."

As the raft slid into the river, George was perched in the front, Brad was on the right side, Brianna was on the left side, and Nate was in the back with Daniella. The inky water was like glass, smooth and tranquil.

"Okay, let's review a few things," said Daniella. "First, I'm guiding this raft. If you don't listen to me, you could put all of us at risk. Until it gets rough, you are free to sit on the sides of the raft. But when I say to get down and sit low, do it. At some places in the rapids we'll have to pull strongly to one side or the other. And sometimes the roar of the water will be deafening. You'll have to strain to hear me. Everyone needs to repeat my instructions out loud so we are all on the same page. Questions, anyone?"

"Got it," replied George. *Just follow the directions.*

"Sounds logical to me," said Brad. *Let's get this show on the road; I've got work to do. Sure hope my shoulder doesn't flare up again.*

"I'm with the team," responded Brianna, her voice a little shaky. *This could be riskier than I thought. I have Abby to think about.*

"Yo, I'm in," chimed Nate. *This looked awesome on the GPS.*

"All right, let's practice a few maneuvers," commanded Daniella. "Nate, take a position behind Brianna. And George, move back in front of Brad."

"Okay, we've got two on the right and two on the left. When I say 'Paddle left,' George and Brad stop paddling; and Brianna and Nate, you guys paddle like your lives depended on it. Reverse it for 'Paddle right.'"

"Paddle right," shouted Daniella. "And remember to repeat the command."

"Paddle right," Nate, Brad, Brianna, and George said in unison. It was a little anemic.

"Shout it loud!" yelled Daniella from the back of the raft.

"PADDLE RIGHT!" screamed the foursome. George and Brad paddled furiously, moving the rubber raft significantly to the right.

"Low in the boat," commanded Daniella.

"Low in the boat!" came the reply, and all four of them slid off the sides and sat down.

"Okay, one last maneuver," said Daniella. "All of you need to be able to get back in the boat if you go overboard. Brianna, let's start with you. Slide out, and I'll show you how to get back in." Before she could protest, Daniella gave Brianna a little nudge, and over she went with a splash.

"Dang, it's cold!" Brianna exclaimed, trying to catch her breath from the shock of the chill. Grabbing the side of the raft, she tried to pull herself up; but her legs slid under the boat, and she looked helpless.

Daniella chuckled. "Okay, good try. Grab onto the raft, and put one leg over. The rest of us will help you roll back inside."

Brianna placed her short, hefty leg on the side of the raft; and, sure enough, it worked—Brad and Nate pulled her in.

George, Brad, and Nate all took turns getting into the water and maneuvering back into the boat. Nate was the only one with enough upper body strength to pull himself in without assistance.

"One final thing," said Daniella. She reached beneath her life jacket, unsnapped a sheath, and pulled out a menacing six-inch hunting knife. "If someone goes overboard and gets trapped under the raft, I have to act quickly. I'll slash the raft and try to pull the person up. I hope that doesn't happen, but I've had to do it before. Questions, anyone?"

Brianna's face was ashen. *All of this for a team-building exercise?*

"All right, let's go!"

Daniella dug her oar strongly in the water and pushed out to the center of the river. *What a motley crew. Oh well, we're in this boat together. Time to experience the real thing.*

Not too far ahead lay the first rapid, "Big Mama," a steep drop and blazing ride through white water, shifting currents, and a challenging obstacle. The team would soon be tested.

PART ONE

Reality of the Rapids

CHAPTER ONE

I'll Guide the Raft

The General Goes to the Helm

The Black River ran through a narrow canyon with steep rock walls on both sides. The scenery was breathtaking. Daniella allowed the group to enjoy the idyllic setting for a few minutes. They would not be able to relax much longer.

"Amazing," said Nate. "Even the GPS satellite couldn't totally capture this."

"I'm jealous," replied Brianna. "I wanted to check out this river via GPS but ran out of time. Abby was cranky last night."

"How do you download GPS on a computer?" asked Brad. *How do these guys have time to mess around on the computer like that? I'm lucky to keep up with my e-mail.*

"Who wants to see it in advance?" quipped George. "The real thrill is the unknown." *I've heard about GPS in cars, but on a computer?*

"Let me describe the first rapid," said Daniella, as she broke into the conversation. "'Big Mama' begins with a sharp vertical drop that will threaten your breakfast. Hang on to your oars. The rapid itself is pretty straightforward. We'll have to navigate around one major boulder and watch for changing currents. It's a good opportunity to get used to the feel of the white water and to learn to function as a team. Remember to repeat each instruction I give you."

Nate let out a yell. "Wicked! Did you guys see that? The raft in front of us just disappeared." George, Brad, and Brianna scanned the river in front of them. Sure enough, the raft that had been five hundred yards ahead was gone from view. "Big Mama" was just ahead.

George gripped his oar tightly and moved slightly closer to the front. "Get ready," he shouted. "Brad, watch out for Brianna! Nate, pay attention."

"Who put you in charge?" demanded Brad; but his question was lost in the sudden roar of the water around them. Although they had been warned, the sheer drop shocked them all. Raging white-foamed water surrounded them. A jagged boulder loomed dead ahead.

"We're going to hit it head on!" screamed Brianna, with panic in her voice.

"Paddle right!" commanded George.

"Paddle LEFT!" shouted Daniella.

"PADDLE LEFT!" repeated the foursome. Brianna and Nate responded immediately. The pull to the left caught a shifting current, and the raft missed the boulder just in the nick of time. The worst was behind them.

"Okay, everyone paddle together," Daniella said in a normal tone of voice. The din of the rapid had diminished. The raft surged ahead, bumped along by the remainder of the rapid. They had some time before the next one.

"George, what happened back there?" demanded Daniella. "Why did you give the command to paddle right?"

"You could have killed us!" shouted Brad.

"It confused me," whined Brianna, still shaken from the precipitous drop.

"Dude, I knew we were supposed to paddle left," said Nate. "The GPS doesn't lie."

George sat there looking sheepish. Wisps of wet white hair lay across his nearly bald head. "Big Mama" had eaten his pork-pie hat. "I don't know what came over me," he replied. "It just seemed natural to take charge, and I was concerned about Brianna. I responded to the adrenaline of the moment without thinking. Sorry."

"You always take charge," said Brad. "It ticks me off. You come off like some sort of general."

"Lighten up, Man," Nate said. "George means well."

"I agree," Brianna chimed in. "I appreciated his asking you to watch out for me."

Daniella was taking it all in. *What a group. Such an age span for four people on one team. No wonder the company sent them on a team-building exercise. Who would be the next to assert their leadership, and what would that look like?* "All right, no harm done," she said. "Let's prepare for the next one. 'Lost Paddle' is coming up fast."

What motivates George, the oldest member of the team and the one who belongs to the Silent Generation? Born between 1925 and 1942, this birth cohort[1] grew up under the dark clouds of the Great Depression and World War II. Although the great majority of this generation missed actual combat duty, these two world-shaking events left an indelible imprint on George's generation.

As Tom Brokaw describes in his book, *The Greatest Generation*, these people grew up during a time of economic despair. A rationing system was in place because of the war effort. Government coupons were required to purchase necessities such as gasoline, shoes, and sugar. Lots of children observed their parents losing homes, businesses, jobs, and farms. Many of them lost fathers, brothers, uncles, and friends in the war.[2] Let that sink in for a moment. When considering the overwhelming effect of such societal occurrences, researchers refer to them as "historically striking events" that shape an entire generation.[3]

The society of George's day was characterized by Judeo-Christian ethics emphasizing a lifestyle of morality, duty, self-denial, and hard work. Integrity and keeping one's word were paramount. Morality mattered. Pregnancy outside of marriage was disgraceful. George's generation married young, and the decision to marry was a lifetime commitment. Men took their role as protector of women seriously.

Business deals were made with a verbal agreement and a firm handshake. A large percentage of society was agrarian, with people living off what they grew on their farms. Communities tended to be small and close-knit, and social functions often revolved around school and church. People helped each other, shared equipment, and pulled together to make ends meet. Doors were not locked.

When George was growing up, people got their news from the radio, which was also how they followed baseball and soap operas. Phone lines were not individual. Several families shared a line, referred to as a "party line," where one could overhear the conversations of others. The first computer had yet to be developed—and when it was, it would fill an entire room.

Growing up in the aftermath of economic scarcity, the Silent Generation tends to be financially conservative and conscious of stewardship. George grew up with a "pay-as-you-go" mentality. No credit cards were available. People saved for what they wanted and paid in cash. The only semblance of credit was found at the general store, where people might "run up a tab," agreeing to pay when the harvest came in or the next payday arrived. Delayed gratification was the norm. George also places a high value on security, planning for the future, and safety.

George was exposed to great leaders who led the nation through difficult times. It was the era of Roosevelt, Patton, and

Eisenhower. Outside of the United States, Winston Churchill was the model, leading the free world in a fight against Hitler and his invading armies. Churchill's motto was "Never, never, never give up!"

This time of executive orders and hierarchy fostered a profound regard for authority. Leadership was characterized by duty, commitment, follow-through, initiative, and morality. A sense of vision and clear calling was evident, because decisions were being made that had implications for years down the road. Leaders in this era focused on getting things done, regardless of the cost. The world of executive leadership was male-dominated, and there was no blurring of the lines between work and home.

George and others in his generation tend to be traditional, conservative, and respectful of authority. In the workplace, these are the people who value job security and benefits and who take pride in what they do, enjoying the satisfaction from a job well done. Organizational loyalty runs high and the command-control approach to management is accepted. The standard leadership model in the Silent Generation was hierarchical, a top-down approach that often created a large gap between the leader and others. But this was recognized; and in fact a more formal employer-employee relationship was expected, and seniority came with age and hard work.[4]

The Georges of today's workforce want to keep working as long as they can, because work is their life. Task and accomplishment are important to them. They will "go to the helm" when necessary and take charge.

"Okay, Daniella, I'm following your lead," said George.

"Glad to hear it," quipped Brad. *Maybe he'll finally resign and get out of my way.*

"What is 'Lost Paddle' like?" asked Brianna. "Any special tips?"

"This one looked awesome," said Nate.

"The only thing I can say is hang on to your paddles!" Daniella said with a laugh. "Here we go!"

CHAPTER TWO

Give Me the Oar

The Boomer Knows Best

In the aftermath of "Big Mama," the team paddled through a patch of calm waters, the polar opposite of their wildly beating hearts. Daniella knew there wasn't much time to regroup. Although it had been scary, the maneuvering required for "Big Mama" was rather simple. That would not be the case with "Lost Paddle."

Brianna noticed it first. "Oh my gosh," she shrieked, "the rocks are everywhere. Which way do we go?"

Daniella rallied the group. "Don't panic! We have to go directly over the rocks, and the water is fast but shallow. We have to choose an outcropping, navigate to it, and everyone will have to use their paddles to push off so that we don't get stuck. Once we're over, the water will just take us, and you can enjoy the ride. Follow my lead!"

George clutched his oar and waited for further instructions. He was not going to repeat the same mistake twice. Nate was clueless. The GPS had revealed the rapid, but it couldn't predict which outcropping would be the best on a given day. Brianna was still numb from "Big Mama."

Brad seized the opportunity. Quickly scanning the various rock formations; the one on the left looked like it had the greatest volume of water. "Let's go left," he hollered. "It has the most water."

Daniella agreed. "Paddle left," came the order.

"PADDLE LEFT!" screamed the group, as they dug their oars into the swift, swirling waters. No current grabbed them this time. They fought to pull the raft to the left. As they approached, the water lifted the raft ever so slightly, and suddenly they were atop the rocks.

Brad felt triumphant. *I was right! I was right! George really blew it back there on "Big Mama." Maybe these guys will finally give me some respect.* Daniella's voice pierced his mental celebration. "Use your paddles to push off," she demanded. "PUSH OFF!"

Brad dug his paddle hard into the rocks. *I'll show them how it's done.*

Brianna, Nate, and George followed suit as each of them pushed against the rocks to nudge the raft forward. The raft suddenly lurched ahead, but Brad's paddle did not. The yellow-handled oar stood upright in the rocks like a flag of triumph. It was solidly wedged in the outcropping.

"Dude, your paddle is history," yelled Nate, as Brad leaned backward, desperately trying to retrieve it. A weird twist of his shoulder yielded a pain with which he was all too familiar. The paddle now belonged to the rapid. "Lost Paddle" had lived up to its reputation, and Brad was the unfortunate one.

"Brad, don't worry about it," said George. "It could have happened to any of us."

"That's right," said Brianna, glad that it had not happened to her.

Nate was already thinking about the next rapid. "Can we make it with one less paddle?"

Daniella observed the responses. *No condemnation. Good. At least they can pull together when they need to.* "Yes, we can make it, but we'll have to be more of a team than ever. Brad, you'll switch off with different ones depending on the rapid."

Brad just sat there. His shoulder hurt. Triumph had so quickly turned to humiliation.

How can one understand Brad, the Baby Boomer of the team? Born between 1943 and 1960, this birth cohort reflects the surge in the birthrate following World War II. When previous census figures are compared, seventeen million extra babies were born.[1]

Early Boomers grew up during a time of educational

expansion. The soldiers had come home from the war and gone back to school. By the time the original GI Bill ended in July 1956, 7.8 million World War II veterans had participated in an education or training program.[2] Optimism was high, vaccines were eradicating childhood illnesses, and most mothers were at home nurturing their children. This generation adopted the idea that they were entitled to the best in life and are often referred to as self-absorbed idealists.[3]

The second wave of Boomers, Brad's group, was born in the mid to late 1950s and grew up in a society undergoing massive change. Gender roles were redefined, the divorce rate escalated, and children began coming home to empty houses—introducing the term "latchkey kid." Television began to take a prominent place in American homes.

A number of "historically striking events," such as the Vietnam War, the Civil Rights Movement, and the sexual revolution shaped the Boomers and rocked the nation. Societal trends began to decline, with higher crime rates and elevated incidences of teenage suicide, drunk driving, illegitimate births, and unemployment. Authority figures no longer enjoyed automatic trust and respect. Boomers developed into strong individualists who emphasized personal rights and freedoms. However, they also matured into people of high responsibility. President Kennedy had challenged this generation with his famous quote, "And so, my fellow Americans: ask not what your country can do for you—ask what you can do for your country."

In the workplace, Boomers, especially those born in the first wave of the boom, are often characterized as workaholics. Being idealists, these folks believe they can make a difference. After all, they are the Baby Boomers! Time is important, time is short; let's make something happen. They are goal- and outcome-oriented and not afraid of hard work. Consequently they are often overachievers and at risk of being driven and spread too thin. Material gain, promotion, titles, and status is emphasized. As one group of authors wrote, "The Boomers invented the 60-hour workweek."[4]

In contrast, last-wave Boomers, like Brad, are characterized as more relaxed and cynical, turned off by the "yuppieism" of their predecessors. They recognize the unhealthiness of a driven lifestyle. Their distrust of authority figures is greater; Boomers definitely want a say in decision making. In terms of work ethic, these Boomers may reflect the attitudes of Generation X more than those held by older Boomers.[5]

Financially, the tendency among Boomers toward immediate gratification led to a spend-now, pay-later mentality, a move away from financial conservatism.[6] This trend represents a significant difference between the Silent and the Boomer generations.

In relation to technology, the computer was coming of age as Boomers grew up. During the 1950s the first programming languages were developed as well as the "chip," or integrated circuit. However, most Boomers were still using punch cards in college, submitting their computer programs and data entry to a large network that transmitted data for evaluation. The phrase "Do not fold, spindle, or mutilate" is indelibly printed in the long-term memories of many Boomers. As technology has taken off, some Boomers have jumped on the learning curve, while others have been reluctant. Most recognize, nevertheless, that constantly changing technology is simply a given in today's working world.

Boomers make up the core membership of numerous associations, attending conferences with a passion, and are ardently involved in the workplace. Many of them are not retiring because they enjoy their work and/or they are not financially able to retire. Others, like Brad, are set to inherit a tidy sum of money from their frugal parents. It is estimated that Boomers will inherit some ten trillion dollars. Many plan to retire early and do other things in life.[7]

The Brads of today's workforce prefer a participatory approach to decision making, creating a level playing field for all. While they are still employed they expect to be key players. They truly believe that a Boomer knows best!

"Okay, folks, the next rapid is intense," Daniella warned. "The 'Bus Stop' does not allow for mistakes. We're going to pull off to the side for a short break so I can give instructions."

"Good idea," responded Nate, who was glad to hear it. He had seen the destructive power of "Bus Stop" on the GPS, and a Skype buddy had related a harrowing story about this rapid. *Sometimes I wish we didn't have so much information available!*

"Nate, you and George paddle us over to the pool of still water on the right," Daniella commanded.

Brad was still silent. *Let's just get this thing over with. I knew my shoulder would flare up again. I wonder what that is gonna cost me.*

As they moved off to the side, Brianna wondered what her role would be.

She would surprise them all.

CHAPTER THREE

Let's Collaborate

Group Decisions Are Better

In the calm of the still water, the group breathed a collective sigh of relief. Not only had they been challenged physically, but "Big Mama" and "Lost Paddle" had also cost them emotionally. Daniella knew they needed to recharge. She anchored her desire to give instructions immediately and remained quiet.

Nate broke the silence. "Okay Daniella, give us the hard, cold facts. I saw the 'Bus Stop' on my computer. It looks evil."

"It's definitely a mean one," replied Daniella. "Let me give you all the game plan. First, you need to have a healthy respect for this rapid. It's called the 'Bus Stop' because its force could literally stop a bus in its tracks. The only way to navigate it is to paddle around one of the edges. If we get sucked into the middle, our raft will just go round and round until the rapid spits us out. Not a pretty picture."

George broke in. "But we are one paddle short. It sounds like we need all the strength we have to paddle around this thing."

Brad just sat there in silence. No eye contact at all.

Brianna observed the nonverbal communiqué. "We can do it. Brad, you can use my paddle. You've got more upper body strength than I do."

Daniella was listening carefully. "What do you all think?" she asked.

"Makes sense to me," said George.

Nate agreed.

Daniella was silent for a moment as she processed internally. *Good teamwork. I'll go with it.* "Okay, let's do that. Brad, you take Brianna's paddle. We need sheer energy to get through this. Brianna, you can help me by making sure the orders are heard."

"Thanks, Brianna," Brad replied in a subdued voice. He was glad to be able to participate. *No need to mention that my shoulder is hurt. No pain, no gain. I can rise above it.*

"Let's paddle back into the stream," Daniella instructed. "We have a short distance to get ready. At my command, paddle with all you've got toward the left edge of the rapid."

Brianna handed her oar to Brad. She had resolved to be the group cheerleader through the rapid. *I'm glad we made the decision as a team.*

George, Nate, and Brad paddled out to the middle and moved the raft downstream.

The first inklings of the "Bus Stop" came not by sight but by sound. Nate was the first to notice. "I think we're getting closer!" he shouted. The roar soon became deafening. And suddenly the rapid came into sight. It resembled the spin cycle of a washing machine. It was a frightening and yet awesome sight to behold. They definitely did not want to get caught in the whirlpool.

"Paddle hard left!" shouted Daniella.

"PADDLE HARD LEFT!" yelled the group, as eager arms dug their oars into the water.

"We can do it!" screamed Brianna, cheering the group on.

As they neared the rapid and headed for the left edge, a weird current caught them, pushing the raft toward the whirlpool of "Bus Stop." "Paddle harder!" commanded Daniella. She knew what could happen.

"PADDLE HARDER!" shrieked the group, energized by adrenalin. George, Nate, and Brad dug their oars even harder into the churning water. At precisely that moment, Brad's shoulder went into a spasm. It was his worst nightmare. He could not perform, and he could not hide it.

"My shoulder is locked up!" Brad cried. "I can't paddle!"

The thunderous roar drowned out his plea. Brianna was still yelling, "We can do it!" when she noticed Brad's discomfort. Quickly sliding forward, she grabbed the oar and shoved it into the water, pulling with all of her might. The extra burst of strength was enough to break free of the funky current. Mercifully, the raft began to pull left. In just the nick of time the group paddled around the left edge, entering an eerily calm patch of water. "Bus Stop" was behind them.

"Brad, what happened back there?" Daniella demanded. "Why did you stop paddling?"

Brad looked as deflated as a week-old balloon. *Why did I ever agree to come on this trip?*

"My shoulder froze up," he replied. "I couldn't paddle. Thanks, Brianna, for coming to my rescue."

George chimed in, "Thanks, Brianna! Great effort. You kept us from being sucked into that rapid!"

Nate added, "Brianna, that was awesome! You gave up your paddle, but you sure knew how to use it when we needed it most."

Daniella's observations continued. *Interesting group. Brianna surprised me. Good effort.* "Okay, let's take a lunch break and regain some energy. We'll need it for the final two rapids. We'll pull out ahead. Brianna, you and George paddle for a few minutes until we reach our lunch site."

Brianna proudly paddled in tandem with George. It felt good to be part of a team.

What motivates Brianna, the Gen X member of the group? Born between 1961 and 1981, Brianna and her generation are the children of the Boomers. Sometimes referred to as Echo Boomers or Baby Busters, this generation grew up in a time of turbulent social change. The divorce rate doubled between 1965 and 1977, leaving many young Gen Xers to grow up in broken homes. Others were raised in families where both parents worked.

A large number of these young people became "latchkey kids," returning at the end of the school day to an empty home in which the television set became the surrogate parent.[1] In fact, the latchkey experience became a defining feature of this generation, allowing for huge amounts of unsupervised time to be filled by the media and popular culture. As one author declared, "This entry into the world of pop culture at such a young age is one reason our generation is unique."[2]

Other societal trends add to the Gen X picture. Some of the highest rates of child poverty, teen suicide, crime, and homelessness in the developed world exist in the United States. These trends did not leave the Gen Xers unscathed. Depression and other emotional problems have surfaced. Numerous authors mention a deep loneliness and a yearning for community in this generation.[3]

Similar to the late-wave Boomers, Brianna witnessed a swiftly changing society—but on a broader scale. The Cold War was replaced by regional wars and terrorist threats. Politically, the Xers grew up in the aftermath of Watergate, the Iran-Contra affair, and the Reagan era. Corporate life experienced a huge paradigm shift. Mergers, downsizing, buyouts, and significant layoffs replaced lifetime employment. Real median wages began falling in the early 1970s. Early in the life of most Xers, America became the world's largest debtor. The economic outlook for Generation X is rather dismal. When they enter their prime earning years, they may very well be paying off the international debt accrued by the Boomers.[4]

In the workplace, Gen Xers tend to have distinct

characteristics that set them apart from the Boomers and the Silents. Although many have described Gen Xers as "slackers," opinions are changing in light of the entrepreneurialism many of these young people are demonstrating. Since they deem company loyalty to be a thing of the past, these young people look to keep their options open; and they are becoming the most entrepreneurial generation in American history.[5]

Gen Xers comprise the first computer generation, excelling in a technological environment characterized by electronic mail, teleconferencing, and multitasking. They have higher levels of education in comparison to previous generations. Xers tend to view the whole idea of career in a very different manner. For them, job-hopping is a way to build skills and become more marketable; self-sufficiency and pragmatism guide the outcomes they seek.

Members of this generation have little patience for bureaucracy and are willing to speak against it; and, if allowed, they can bring fresh perspective and life into corporations. Like their Boomer parents, the Xers are cautious of authority. Unlike the Silent Generation, where respect was automatically ascribed to age, position, or time with the company, Gen Xers develop trust and give respect when it is earned. The qualification is authentic character and integrity.[6]

Technology itself has contributed to the culture gap between Xers and their Boomer and Silent predecessors. Computer literacy is a defining feature of this generation, and digital imaging allows for incredible personal expression. Most notable is the ability to blur fantasy and everyday experience. Popular movies like *The*

Matrix and video games illustrate this trend.[7]

Financially, the Xers have continued in the Boomer footsteps of personal debt. In fact, they have been raised to believe that they are entitled to the same things their parents had—but instantly. This generation carries more personal debt at their age than any other generation in the history of the United States. Gen Xers wonder if they will ever collect Social Security. They tend to live for the moment. The "pay-as-you-go" mentality of George's day has been replaced by "buy now and pay later," both at the personal and the national level.[8]

The Briannas of today's workforce are highly creative, technologically gifted, and motivated. Having witnessed the unbalanced lives of their parents, however, this generation tends to assume the position of working to live—rather than living to work. Thus they prefer to operate smart, utilizing a more flexible schedule, with a focus on getting the job done and maintaining a boundary between work and personal life.

They also desire training, mentoring, variety, and continued opportunities for personal development. Management that wants to keep the Gen Xers around will be inclusive and relational and will allow for flexibility and innovation.[9]

"There's our lunch spot," Daniella said as she pointed to a small sandy patch alongside the river. "Paddle over, pull the raft out, and let's get something to eat."

Brad said nothing. *I feel sick to my stomach.*

"I'm all for that," replied Nate, whose stomach was demanding food.

George and Brianna were ready to eat too.

Daniella stepped out of the raft and watched as the team pulled it out. Nate's physical strength was obvious. *I wonder what he has on the inside? "Disaster Falls" and "Table Saw" will sure reveal it.*

Nate was devouring a sandwich, oblivious to what loomed ahead.

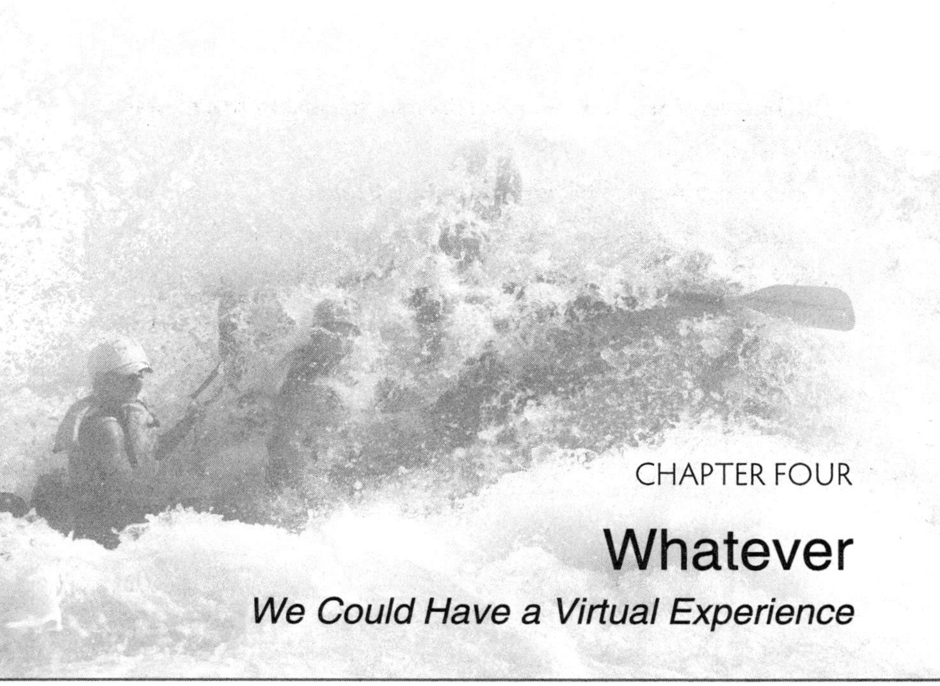

CHAPTER FOUR

Whatever

We Could Have a Virtual Experience

Daniella gave the team another fifteen minutes to digest their food and to regroup. They would need all the energy those carbs could provide. Two final rapids awaited them before this team-building exercise was over. Although the group had already been tested significantly, nothing compared to "Disaster Falls" and "Table Saw." She sat in silence, mentally assessing their strengths and weaknesses. *It's too bad that we are one man down. Strength is what we need at this point.*

Nate broke through her contemplation. "When do we shove off?" he asked. "I'm stoked about the rest of the river; it looked gnarly on the computer. Lots of speed in this next rapid. Let's roll!"

Brad cast a cold stare in his direction. *Showoff. Just like at the office. He thrives on excitement. It's the steady guys like me that get the job done. Gnarly is how I feel. I'd give anything if this team-building thing were just over.*

Nate caught the nonverbal message and shrugged his shoulders nonchalantly. *What is his problem? Whatever, Dude. I'm not the slacker you think I am.*

George and Brianna were quiet. Their energy levels were waning like tires slowly losing air.

"You're right, Nate," Daniella responded. "'Disaster Falls' *is* fast. Okay everyone, listen up. I can tell you are getting tired, but we need to pull together to navigate the final two rapids. We've got at least another hour of work ahead of us."

Brianna breathed deeply. *C'mon girl, you can do it.*

George sat up straight and gripped his oar tightly. *I may be older, but I can still hold my own. Heck, I'm doing better than Brad, and he's my son's age.*

Daniella continued. "We've got about ten minutes ahead of us that is calm. Just paddle and enjoy. The next rapid is named after the waterfall that feeds into the river. Gorgeous to look at, but dangerous. Lots of fast white water that can toss you out of the raft and into the rocks. Not a good combination. Stay focused. At my command you'll have to really dig your oars at certain times to nudge the raft in one direction or another. And remember the command about getting low in the boat. We may need it. Questions, anyone?"

No one said a word, but a common thought flowed through each of their minds. *I sure hope she doesn't have to use that hunting knife.*

"Okay, push off," Daniella commanded. Brad, you're back here with me. Give your shoulder a rest."

Nate pushed the raft back into the water as the group climbed in to take their positions. George, Brianna, and Nate paddled as they lazily passed by relaxing scenery.

The calm water allowed for some conversation. Brianna began. "Why do you guys think they sent us on this exercise? Is something up that I don't know about?"

"I'm clueless," replied Nate, "although there's been some internal e-mail chatter about other teams scheduled for team building too."

Brad chimed in. "I've been wondering if something is up. This kind of activity is not normal for Handover. Too touchy-feely for the founder. But I've noticed that transition seems to be in the air."

George joined in. "Don't be too surprised. Mr. White is more open to change than you think. He sees global trends and responds. Team building is really popular these days."

The roar of the waterfall brought their dialogue to an end. The water plunging into the river was impressive. White water replaced the calm waters they had just navigated, and it was swift.

Daniella issued her first directive. "Nate, take the forward position and watch for rock outcroppings. George, you and Brianna stay on the sides and pull at my command. Brad, stay back here with me. If I have to assist someone, you'll have the rudder."

Suddenly the ride became tumultuous. White-water swells engulfed the raft. Visibility was nearly impossible in every direction. As Daniella opened her mouth to shout "Low in the boat," a wave of water surged over the right side of the raft, and in an instant Brianna was overboard.

George spotted her orange life jacket. "She's over there!" he yelled.

Daniella screamed to Brianna, "Keep your legs up and ride it out!" But it was too late. She disappeared right in front of their eyes.

Danielle's knife was of no use now. Brianna wasn't under the raft. In fact, their black rubber craft was quickly leaving her behind as the white water propelled them forward. Suddenly, without question or comment, Nate released his life jacket and plunged into the swirling whirlpool.

Daniella scanned for a large rock formation where they could hold tight. No way. The raft surged ahead and wouldn't find a resting place until beyond the rapid. George, Brad, and Daniella bumped along in silence, sitting low in the boat to ride out the remaining swells. The two guys were in shock, and for once Daniella was speechless.

Under the black, swirling waters, Nate strained for a glimpse of Brianna. *I've got to find her.* The current was random, pushing him against sharp rocks that slashed at his extremities. He surfaced for another gulp of air and scanned. Nothing. *She has a life jacket on. Why isn't she floating somewhere?* The only plausible conclusion formed in a nanosecond in his brain. *She's trapped by a rock. Oh God, help me! It's already been a couple of minutes.* He dove down again.

Suddenly, miraculously, something brushed against his foot. A strap. He grabbed it and kicked toward its source, Brianna's orange life vest. She looked limp, with her left arm stuck between two rocks that held her just centimeters beneath the oxygen source above. Nate steadied himself, reached under her head, and gently lifted it above the surface to get air. He would have to work on the arm in a minute.

Brianna gasped for air like a newborn fresh from the womb. She coughed violently, vomited, and gulped the oxygen again. She was alive.

"Stay calm, Brianna. I've got to free your arm." She was obviously in pain.

"Look, I know this is scary, but I've got to let go of your head so I can work on your arm that's stuck. Take a deep breath and go back under. I'll keep you coming up for air every minute or so."

Brianna wanted to protest, but almost involuntarily she took a big breath and allowed Nate to lower her head under the black waters. *I've got to get free. My Abby needs me.*

Nate squinted in the water to see how to free her left arm. The space between the rocks provided a perfect fit for Brianna's arm. Too perfect—it was tight. His brain whipped through multiple solutions like a computer processor at warp speed, and suddenly an image came back to his attention. He had seen a rescue like this on a video game. He and Brianna came back up for air.

"Brianna, hang in there. I think I've got a solution," panted Nate, who was gasping for air himself. "I'm going to need your life jacket."

No protest from Brianna. Just a quiet comment: "Please hurry; I'm getting really cold."

I wonder if she's going into shock. Nate shook off the thought and lowered her head once again. He removed Brianna's life jacket and quickly wrapped the strap around one of the rocks holding her in its vise. As the orange vest floated to the surface, Nate jerked hard on the strap, loosening the rock just enough to pull Brianna's arm free. He grabbed the vest, put his arm around Brianna's waist, and both of them came up for air.

The white water still swirled around them. "Brianna, put your legs up, and we'll ride this thing out!" Nate shouted.

Brianna was shivering and definitely in autopilot mode. Nate put her arm through one side of the vest, and he took the other. They laid on their backs, floating with the help of the vest, and began to move through the rapid.

Five minutes later, the longest five minutes of Nate's life, the worst was behind them.

Brad spotted them first. "There they are!" he screamed with real emotion. He wasn't thinking about his shoulder anymore.

Daniella let out a sigh of relief.

George's eyes filled with tears.

Brad and George paddled over to the twosome, and Daniella helped pull them in, noticing the cuts and bruises that "Disaster Falls" had left on Brianna and Nate. Brianna looked pale, and Nate leaned against the raft, breathing a prayer of thanks.

Brad leaned over and put his hand on Nate's shoulder. "You saved Brianna's life. It took guts to do what you did. You've got more on the inside than I've ever seen before."

Nate grinned. The generational divide melted like ice cream on a hot summer day.

"Take the raft over to the left side of the river," barked Daniella, who was fully in control once more. "Let's see what we need to finish the course." *We may have to skip the last rapid.*

For once no one disagreed or copped an attitude. They were safe and glad to be alive—Glad to be in the boat together.

What inspires Nate, the youngest member of the team, who belongs to the Millennial Generation—those born between 1982 and twenty years thereafter? According to Howe and Strauss, the Millennial Generation is clearly the largest cohort in history, the result of a flood of thirty-something Boomers who finally decided to become parents and of Gen Xers who were also having children at the same time.[1]

Perhaps the word that best captures this generation is "wanted." These kids have been chauffeured around in minivans with "Baby on Board" bumper stickers. Precious cargo sat in those vehicles, complete with child safety seats and protective door locks. Parents have been protective, and their children have been sheltered.[2]

Parents sought the best education for their children, evaluating options carefully and making sacrifices for private schools when deemed necessary. Extracurricular activities have been the norm. Harried parents have juggled life between working and shuttling their little ones to soccer, piano, ballet, karate, baseball, and a myriad of other activities. The Millennials have been the busiest generation of kids we've ever seen, dealing with carefully planned schedules that used to be reserved for adults. Many of their activities have been competitive, but a different attitude has prevailed. In this birth cohort, "Everyone is a winner." Self-esteem has been of utmost importance.[3] These trends continue today and do not seem to be diminishing.

Pressured to study hard and capitalize on opportunities, many of these Millennials are quite confident and optimistic. Countless others feel stressed and overwhelmed by options. Although Howe and Strauss hailed this group as the next "hero" generation that will be committed to civic spirit, teamwork, and community, others describe them as skeptical, uncivil, and disengaged.[4]

In an article entitled *Generation NeXt Comes to College*, this cohort is characterized as the ultimate consumer, expecting high grades with little effort, demanding luxury and comfort, having low respect for authority, and becoming defensive when confronted by constructive criticism.[5] Instant gratification is the mantra of the society in which this generation has grown up, with the prevailing attitude that it truly is all about them. This is the same generation, however, that has demonstrated a new surge of volunteerism, especially in times of great need. With the click of a mouse they can mobilize their peers for action.[6]

An economic boom marked Nate's teenage years as his

generation witnessed a skyrocketing stock market, the rise of technology-based companies, and a revitalized market economy. He also saw the economic bubble burst in 2000, right before his graduation from high school. College expenses have soared. Costs for one year at a public university now average about twelve thousand dollars. Many of these young people graduate with massive student loans that may take a lifetime to repay.[7]

Yet for Nate and many of his friends, a college education was not an option. Their parents expected it. It is estimated that one-third of the Millennials will complete a university education, which is a higher proportion of the cohort than for Generation X or the Boomers. Though higher education comes at a high price, it is the ticket to a better job and income. Unfortunately, educational debt will not be the only economic barrier to this generation. Mortgages, health care costs, tax burdens, and childcare expenses for two-income families have all soared. The children of the Boomers are now the new class of debtors. Debt has become the norm; it is simply accepted by this generation.[8]

Not only are these young people graduating with a load of debt, but many also have difficulty entering the workforce with success because of an inability to think long-term, handle details, or delay gratification.[9] In *TIME Magazine's* January 24, 2005 cover story, entitled "Meet the Twixters," Lev Grossman describes a delayed entry into adulthood with young people moving back in with their parents, bouncing from job to job, and hopping from partner to partner.

Divorce rates have continued to be high, and this generation has witnessed a redefinition of family. The original nuclear family of George's generation is only one of many Millennial models that include single parents, blended families, and same-sex partnerships. Smoking has become fashionable in this age group. This generation is also known for "clubbing," combining alcohol use with the use of recreational drugs such as Ecstasy, methamphetamine ("ice"), and crack cocaine.[10]

The Millennials witnessed the events of September 11, 2001, another "historically striking" incident that altered life as they knew it. An official "war on terrorism" opened the twenty-first century. Their generation has witnessed two wars with Iraq, the Taliban toppled in Afghanistan, and many reports of potential nuclear proliferation in places like North Korea and Iran. They cannot peruse Internet news without being confronted with issues like global warming, shortages of oil and clean water sources, HIV/AIDS, and an increasingly globalized economy with its demands for innovation and competition. They have learned that the world is a dangerous place.

Technologically, this generation is in the fast lane of the information superhighway. Often referred to as the "Net Generation," this is the first true Internet cohort. The Millennials prefer interactive media, which is evidenced by the exponential growth of blogging, e-mail, streaming video, ubiquitous cell phones and text messaging, and websites like MySpace and Facebook where people meet anonymously online. Internet dating is commonplace. These young people have never lived without cable television. Instant global communication is standard, yielding a potent culture of interaction that can mobilize and inform millions in a short time. The world of the Millennials is rapidly changing.[11]

In the workplace, these young people are eager for a variety of experiences and hesitate to make long-term commitments. They prefer to commit to a string of short-term assignments, which gives them freedom and flexibility. Similar to Generation X, large numbers of Millennials desire to start their own business and work for themselves. If they work for others, they easily multitask, prefer an inclusive form of leadership, and need lots of feedback. They are innovative, technologically talented, and good team players—but they bore easily. Work should be interesting, stimulating, and lead to advancement. Like their Gen X predecessors, Millennials don't automatically give respect but look for integrity, authenticity, and understanding. They are currently streaming into the workplace and will fill a big void as Boomers retire.[12]

Daniella's little band of rafters leaned against the sides of the rubber boat like whipped puppies sprawled on a porch during a hot summer afternoon. A slight smile crept across her face as she scanned the crew. *They really put in a good effort, and I think they learned some things about one another that they had never known before. It's enough.*

No one said a word.

This time it was Daniella who broke the silence. "Folks, you have put in an incredible effort, but there is no way we can tackle the final rapid. We are too depleted."

A weak grin split Nate's face as he quipped, "Whatever. I'll show you guys 'Table Saw' on the GPS back at the office."

George, Brad, and Brianna nodded in agreement. All four knew they couldn't go any farther.

"George, you stay here with Nate and Brianna. Brad, you come with me. We need to hike about a mile down the road and retrieve the bus. We'll come back for the rest of you and the equipment."

Brad sat up straight, feeling useful again, and quickly stepped out of the raft to join Daniella. *This lady wasn't so bad after all.*

As they turned to leave, Daniella unzipped a pouch on her jacket, extracted four Swiss chocolate bars, and handed them to the rafters. "I usually save these for the end, but enjoy. We'll be back within an hour."

Brianna cried at the kindness. *I almost died back there. I can't wait to get home.*

Forty-five minutes later, the threesome with the raft heard the grinding gears of the aged bus. Their chariot had arrived, and they were ready to ride.

"Woo hoo!" shouted George, as the yellow bus came into view. Tears still rolled down Brianna's face. Nate placed his arm around her shoulder and gave her a quick hug. "It's okay."

It didn't take long to load the raft, oars, and life jackets into the back of the bus. This group was ready to go home. They stepped onboard and rode in silence back to the original launch site.

"One last thing, announced Daniella. You missed the photo

finish scheduled after 'Table Saw.' We had a photographer set up to capture the moment. So let's take a minute for a quick team shot."

"Let's get a couple of paddles and life jackets for the pic," shouted Nate. He was springing back to life.

Brad let out a groan but cooperated.

The foursome lined up in front of the yellow behemoth painted with the Black River Rafting logo and smiled. Nate held an oar high above his head, sporting a triumphant expression. George put on a life jacket and grinned. Brianna mustered a smile. Brad sucked in his stomach and looked stoic.

Click. The team-building exercise was over, and they had a photo to prove it.

As they thanked Daniella and loaded into their cars, they had no idea that another series of rapids was waiting for them back at the office. They would need every skill they had just learned in order to survive and remain in the boat together.

PART TWO

Formation of a Rapid

CHAPTER FIVE

Turbulence

Four Streams Merging

The weekend was boring in comparison to what each of them had experienced the day before. Shopping at Wal-Mart could not compare to Big Mama, Disaster Falls, Bus Stop, and Lost Paddle, although trying to find just the right checkout lane did seem similar to navigating a rapid!

Nate blogged the whole experience; Brianna spent extra time with her daughter, Abby; Brad watched sports on television; and George worked outdoors in his yard. Each of them reflected on their common experience, feeling quite connected to one another and looking forward to being back together at the office. After all, they had been through a lot together. Maybe some other working groups should do a rafting trip together—minus the near-death experience, of course.

Monday morning came soon enough. Nate was the first to get the e-mail. His BlackBerry beeped at seven o'clock, notifying him of incoming mail. He didn't like to wait to check mail on the office terminal. The subject line of the e-mail seized his attention: "Changeover at Handover." *Catchy. What does that mean?*

Brianna downloaded her e-mail in the car after dropping Abby off at preschool. Cell phones were great for multitasking. The Handover e-mail jolted her. She swerved to avoid a car that had stopped in front of her. *What is up now?* She couldn't handle much more. *What more does this company want from me? I almost died the other day.*

Brad stopped at Starbucks on the way to the office. He was still feeling sluggish and humiliated after the momentous rafting expedition. "Make it a venti this morning," he said, "and a double shot of espresso." *I need some caffeine.* He pulled into the parking lot at Handover and ambled to the office. He was in no rush to check e-mail. More and more, it seemed like a curse. His inbox was never empty. He logged in. The e-mails streamed onto his screen as he sipped his espresso and perused them. He had just noticed the e-mail marked for priority, "Changeover at Handover," when Nate IM'd him: "Dude, did you read the big news yet?" Brad was not amused. He only had about seven years before early retirement. *Why can't I finish my time at Handover in peace?*

George was the last to get the news. He had gotten to the office early but was already busy with a hardware repair. He preferred the old style of communication: staff meeting or flyer posted on the wall. Brianna printed a copy of the e-mail for him and took it to his workspace.

"Seen this yet, George?"

"What is it?" he replied.

"Company communiqué," Brianna said. "Listen to the subject line: Changeover at Handover."

"Well, I guess I'd better read it," George said as he laid a micro screwdriver down. *I've seen so many changes over the years; it can't be that bad.*

One by one they all read the same thing:

> Attention all employees of Handover Corp. This is to notify you that after fifty years of leading the company that I started in my basement, the time has come for me to retire and hand the reigns of leadership to someone else. Transition of leadership is never easy, but we will endeavor to make it as smooth as possible. An outside firm has been hired to help identify possible candidates for CEO. In the meantime I have appointed an interim CEO, Dr. Daniel Batten, from our West Coast office. Our first meeting with Dr. Batten will be on Wednesday at 9:00 A.M. Please be prompt. Thank you for your loyal service.
>
> Edward C. White, founder and CEO, Handover Corp.

By now the four of them—Brad, Brianna, Nate, and George—were gathered in George's workspace. Brad was the most irritated. "Why do we need an interim CEO? That will make the transition doubly hard. I know that Daniel Batten is with Handover, but he works in an entirely different division. He has no history with our situation. I have a bad feeling about this."

Nate chimed in. "Well, he can bring in some objectivity. He's an outsider."

Brianna agreed.

George's take on it was typical. "Hey, Mr. White knows what he's doing. He has things under control. Don't worry."

The day passed with a flurry of e-mails flying back and forth among the three hundred employees at Handover. Speculation abounded. *Would anyone lose his or her job? How would Edward White's successor be chosen—from inside the company or from the outside? How soon would the changeover take place? How would this affect the value of the company stock?*

The questions were endless, and emotions were rising. *Would the company be reorganized? What about the pension program? What would happen to individual departments? What might middle management look like? Would office space remain the same?*

Wednesday finally arrived. There was no problem with people being late that day. At 9:00 A.M. the large conference room was jam-packed, and a buzz filled the room. Edward White, founder and CEO, stepped up to the podium. His snow-white hair and creased face reminded everyone of his age. Instant silence.

"Friends and coworkers," he began, "this meeting today is historic. By January 1 of next year, I will no longer be the CEO of this company. I will always be the founder, of course, but the time has come for me to step aside and let a new generation of leadership take charge. Globalization is changing the face of business, and we must change with the times. This changeover is not only about my stepping aside. It's also a complete reexamination of our structure, leadership, communication systems, and productivity. We've hired the best to lead us through the process of finding my successor. Until that person is identified, Dr. Daniel Batten has agreed to serve as the interim CEO and my personal advisor. He will be reviewing every department and making recommendations for change in preparation for the leadership transition. Daniel is one of our own, so please welcome him warmly."

A solid round of applause filled the room. Daniel Batten, a thin, wiry man who looked to be in his mid-fifties, launched immediately into an overview of Handover Corp.—its inception, history, and productivity over the years. He spoke eloquently about Edward White's company vision and accomplishments. Finally, he leaned his slender frame over the podium and cut to the chase. Big changes were needed. Handover Corp. needed to be reorganized to allow for greater profit margin, greater productivity, and increasing competition. Each department would be reviewed, beginning with the IT group, which included software design, computer security, website development, and hardware. They would meet on Friday afternoon.

George, Nate, Brad, and Brianna felt as if they just hit "Big Mama" all over again. That stomach-churning feeling was all too familiar.

As the foursome met for lunch that day, the conjecture began. "Well, folks," began Brad, "it's obvious. IT is the key to the future. They should expand this department and give each one of us additional staff members. And it's about time. We have been understaffed for too long."

Brianna wasn't so sure. "I don't know. Webpage design can be outsourced. So can software, Brad. I wonder if I'll be here next month. Bummer—I just became vested in the 401K plan." *We're already in debt up to our eyeballs.* She stared into the distance, a glazed look on her face.

Nate was searching Google for transitions of medium-sized companies and for background information on Daniel Batten. "Hard to tell," he said. "Not much information about this guy. But current business trends are about globalization, e-commerce, technology, and integration."

George joined the discussion. "How do you integrate hardware repair and software design?" *All I know is I just want to keep working.*

Early Friday afternoon Daniel Batten showed up at the IT department. What he had to say shocked them all. "George, Brad, Brianna, Nate," he began, "each of you has done a good job in your respective area. However, this group has functioned like a swim team, with each one tackling his or her own lane. The key to the future is strategic integration."

Nate smiled. *Google tells all.*

Brad's eyebrows went up. "How do you integrate security, software, webpage design, and hardware maintenance?" he quipped.

Batten didn't blink an eye. "That's what we're going to work on." He continued. "We're going to take a fresh look at your unit. I'm designating Brianna as the department leader, and she will report directly to me. She and I will meet Monday to review the IT operation for Handover. I expect your full cooperation. Any questions?"

No one said a word. It was like "Disaster Falls" all over again. Who might go overboard this time? Next week would be interesting. That was an understatement.

CHAPTER SIX

Big Mama

Authority and Respect

The Friday afternoon commute was a blur to Brianna, barely registering in her long-term memory. Although she navigated her way home, it was simply by reflex. Her mind whirred like a hard drive crunching data. *Why did they put me in charge? Why not Brad? He has far more seniority. I hope they're not expecting a miracle. What if I can't deliver? I'm not going to work night and day for this company. I have a little girl, for goodness sake.*

Cruising down another route, Nate listened to his favorite XM radio station, guided home by the soothing female voice on his GPS system. *Things are sure going to get interesting at work.*

I wonder what Brad is thinking. I wouldn't want to be in the lane next to him. A slight grin crossed his face. *Whatever. The weekend awaits. I'll deal with it on Monday.*

Road rage dominated Brad's commute. He was ticked off. *Brianna was right. This transition is all about downsizing. And I'm being skipped over. Why in the world would company management bypass all of my years of experience? If I had my hands on that inheritance money. . . .* The sound of screeching tires and the smell of burning rubber jerked his attention back to the road. He shot an irate glance at the driver behind him and raised a fist in protest. *I can't believe I've got to report to Brianna. I need a beer.*

George drove his normal route home, unperturbed and looking forward to dinner. He too listened to the radio. In fact, his favorite country-western song was playing at that very moment, and he joined in, crooning like the best of them. A song about the strength of a woman. *Yep, that's my wife. Just another change at work. I can get through anything with her by my side. Besides, I like Brianna. I'm so glad she didn't drown.*

Monday morning came all too soon. Brianna decided to get to the office early to collect her thoughts before Brad, George, and Nate met in her office at nine. She had asked them to meet with her before she met with Daniel Batten. *I'm already sweating. Calm down, girl. Take a few deep breaths. Teamwork. Focus on teamwork. I need these guys.*

George ambled in at 8:55. "Morning, Brianna," he said cheerily. "How was your weekend?"

"A little stressful," Brianna replied. "This transition really weighed on my mind. Kyle kept telling me to chill out, but Abby helped take my mind off of work."

Nate bounded through the office door right at nine. "Hey, Boss!" he quipped.

Brianna grimaced. "Well, I guess I wouldn't be in this position if you hadn't saved my life," she joked in return.

"Has anyone seen Brad?" Brianna asked, looking at the clock. It wasn't like him to be late.

Ten minutes later Brad charged through the door with latte in hand. He plopped heavily into a chair. "Mornin' all," he said through pursed lips. The tension was palpable.

Nate categorized it immediately. *I think I notice some passive-aggressive behavior here.*

"Dude, is that decaf or the real thing? I don't think you need any more caffeine."

Brad shot him a look that could kill.

"Okay everyone, let's get started," said Brianna, her voice almost an octave higher than normal. "I wanted to meet together before Daniel Batten outlines the project to me."

"Look," she continued, her intonation returning to normal, "this whole thing is really awkward for me. I didn't expect this turn of events, and I feel overwhelmed and nervous, just like when we hit 'Big Mama.' My stomach has been in turmoil since Friday."

"I don't know much about integration," said George. "But I'll help in any way I can. You have my support."

"Thanks, George," replied Brianna, breathing a sigh of relief.

He could be my grandfather. It feels bizarre to be the department leader.

She continued. "This whole thing is a real challenge, but if we do it together, it can be fun. We could actually make a difference. I mean, we survived 'Disaster Falls,' didn't we?"

Nate responded immediately. "I'm with you, Brianna. I don't know what all this will lead to; but if we stick together, we can make it." A broad smile spread across his face. "I'll share a life jacket with you again."

A big grin split Brianna's face.

"Brad, what about you?" she asked, gaining confidence from the others. *Maybe we really can work as a team.*

Brad cleared his throat. "Brianna, nothing personal against you, but I think this whole thing is a bunch of crap. It really ticks me off."

Nate jumped into the conversation. He had some anger of his own. "What do you mean, it's not personal? Get real! You would rather be the leader, wouldn't you?"

Brad's neck turned red, his jugular vein throbbed, and the crimson streak was headed to his face. He could restrain himself no longer.

"This transition is a farce," he exploded, his voice many decibels louder than normal. "Let me tell you what it is *really* all about."

Brianna's face was ashen.

Brad gulped some air and continued. "Downsizing. Getting rid of unnecessary people. Bigger profits. What a bunch of crap. Edward White cared about people. Who knows what the new leadership will be like? It makes me sick."

At that precise moment, Daniel Batten knocked on the door.

"Come in," said Brianna weakly.

"Everything okay in here?" Batten asked. "I could hear you guys all the way down the hall."

Silence.

"Fine, just fine," replied Brad, sitting with his arms folded tightly across his chest.

"Brianna, let's meet in ten minutes, okay?" Daniel Batten remained standing at the door. *Minefield. I'm not getting any closer.*

"Okay, I'll be there," responded Brianna.

Batten closed the door behind him.

"Let's get together again this afternoon over coffee," Brianna said with a subdued voice. *How embarrassing that we were heard down the hall. What do they expect from me? I didn't ask for this assignment—Brad can have it.*

George, Brad, and Nate agreed to come back at three o'clock. She sighed as they filed out of her office. Brianna had five minutes to regroup before meeting with Batten. The week had just begun, but she was already exhausted.

Authority and respect—two words that used to be self-explanatory, especially in George's generation. Whoever was in charge commanded respect. It was automatic. No questions asked. The command-and-control model of leadership prevailed in the 1940s and 1950s, a time marked by military service. People who grew up in that generation describe leadership with words such as *general, boss, strong, authoritarian*, and *military*. They also talk about *duty, commitment, perseverance*, and *morality*.[1] In a large research study, leaders in this cohort identified "listens well," "credible," "delegates," and "dedicated" as their top four descriptions of leadership.[2]

From the perspective of this generational cohort, there is a big gap between the boss and others; this is understood and considered normal. Leaders take the helm. As one executive put it, "I think the WWII generation was clearly Eisenhower, strong leadership, Patton, the general knows to go to the helm. I think the Boomers reacted to that a great deal, but I don't think we changed it. Especially not the early end of the Baby Boomers."[3]

Although some shifts in thinking appear to have taken place in the Boomer generation, behavior has often remained similar to that of the Silent Generation, especially by the early Boomers. These folks are characterized as workaholics who are concerned with material gain, promotion, title, and status. Within the Boomer cohort, especially among the older ones, leadership is still described as *responsibility, duty, loyalty, control, obligation*, and *driven*. Although they prefer a more collaborative leadership style, older Boomers remain goal- and outcome-oriented as they climb the ladder to the top.[4] When they reach it, the helm is theirs, and they are the decision makers.

However, the late-wave Boomers reflect a definite change in orientation toward leadership and authority figures in general.

These are the Brads who grew up with the saying, "Don't trust anyone over thirty." These Boomers question authority and may tend to be cynical and angry. They want to be included in major decisions and have the freedom to disagree. One Boomer leader captured it succinctly: "I respect the position, but if we come to the table, we are minds coming together to discuss what is happening. . . . I need to be able to totally disagree and need to be able to say that, in my opinion, I think they are messing up."[5]

Imagine the shock when leaders from the Silent Generation are questioned about their decisions. Such posturing from those who are younger can be interpreted as disloyalty, disunity, or outright rebellion. On the flip side, younger leaders are equally shocked when their thoughts and feelings are not considered in the process. They may feel frustrated, used, left out, or rejected. A potent streak of individualism runs through the Boomer generation and continues unabated in the younger cohorts.

In fact, this trend toward collaboration and cautious respect is even more pronounced among the Gen Xers and Millennials. Their attitude toward authority and organizational loyalty is light years away from George's generation. The Xers and Millennials may defer to those in authority, but true respect, from their perspective, is earned.[6]

Consider a few comments from leaders in these two cohorts (names have been changed):

- "It doesn't depend on their age; it depends how they handle their age, how they see themselves as a leader

. . . how they live out their leadership." —Tony, age twenty-five

- "I defer to leaders who are older than me, but I check what they say. . . . I definitely look up to leaders that are older than me, but they don't automatically have my respect. They have to have a character that I can respect." —John, age twenty-eight
- "I tend to evaluate them—listening to them, asking them questions, seeing where they are coming from. Also what I can draw from them. . . . I check them out." —Bob, age forty
- "If I see their character, and I'm impressed and attracted to it, then I am attracted to them. If I see flaws or something I can't respect, I don't care to know them or be under them." —Sally, age thirty-three
- "I get a little uncomfortable, to be honest. It depends on who they are. If they are approachable and I can be myself, then it is okay. But if I feel like they don't have time, I get really insecure." —Janet, age twenty-eight[7]

These types of comments point to one word: relationship. Leaders may get obedience, but respect comes out of relationship. What does that look like in the workplace? People want to be included in decision making, especially when major changes are being considered. In one research study, late-wave Boomers and all Gen Xers indicated a high desire for feedback.[8] Of course, this requires getting to know people and taking the time to listen to them. It involves mentoring and caring. As these behaviors are practiced, the gap between the leaders and the employees is narrowed.

One Gen Xer, age twenty-seven, shared his thoughts on leadership and relationship very poignantly:

> After the last set of national leadership meetings I attended, I came home and cried for forty minutes because the focus was on all the problems. And I thought, if this is what leadership is about, I don't want to do this. I want to be out there doing stuff that affects people instead of worrying about buildings and money. . . . The fathers are there to support us. I don't think you can bypass spending time with an older person; getting to know them on an individual basis is priceless. How can we spend time with some of these leaders? . . . That is my heart's plea.[9]

Authority and *respect* are words that will appear the same in a dictionary, whether used by George, Brad, Brianna, or Nate. The real meaning and interpretation of those concepts, however, are as varying as a river rapid. Understanding these differences and working with them can alter the atmosphere in the workplace, allowing for consideration, unity, greater relationship, and, ultimately, more productivity.

Five minutes were up. As Brianna trudged down the hall to meet with Daniel Batten, memories of the gut-wrenching drop of "Big Mama" flooded her mind. His words would not offer much comfort.

CHAPTER SEVEN

Disaster Falls

Leadership Styles

What happened in there?" Daniel Batten asked, as he began his meeting with Brianna to review the IT department.

"I don't really know," Brianna replied, looking sheepish. "Everything was going great, and then I asked Brad for his thoughts. He exploded. It really caught me off guard and shook me up."

Batten smiled knowingly. "Get used to it. Part of leadership. Brad is probably angry about reporting to you. He won't be any happier after he hears about the new plan."

Brianna didn't respond. *That's just great. What did I do to deserve this new position?*

"Okay, let's begin," continued Batten. "I'm not going to sugarcoat the situation. We are losing money and need to look at how to become more profitable. With the company entering transition with Mr. White's planned resignation, we have the freedom to try some new things. I want to look at some outsourcing."

Brianna struggled to keep her composure. "Which areas do you think we can outsource?" *Brad was right. I can't believe it. I'm being asked to help people lose their jobs.*

"Well, we are going to begin with IT, especially with software design," Batten replied. "Parts of India are the new 'Silicon Valley.' We can send projects to them, go home for the night, and have results the next day. And we'll save untold thousands of dollars."

"That's Brad's area," groaned Brianna.

"I know," Batten said. "But we are not going to let Brad go, at least not for the time being. We can use him to monitor quality when the software code comes in."

"What else?" queried Brianna, already dreading the response.

"I also want to outsource hardware maintenance," replied Batten. "We can contract with a local firm for that."

"And what happens to George?" Brianna demanded.

"We'll offer him a nice severance package," quipped Batten. "He's already past retirement age anyway."

Now it was Brianna's turn to react. "Who decided all of this?" she asked with an edge in her voice that surprised her. "It doesn't sound like Edward White to me."

"It's my call, Brianna," declared Batten. "I am the acting CEO. I'm trying to get some things in order before the new person comes on board. What's the problem?"

"I don't get it," Brianna said. "Handover sent our IT team on a team-building exercise that almost cost me my life. What's the point of dumping George and eventually eliminating Brad? We're in a better position to work together than ever before."

A wry smile crossed Batten's face. "Don't you think I got a report from that trip? You and Nate rose to the top. I'm looking for new leadership, and you're it."

Suddenly Brianna felt as trapped as when she was pinned under the rocks at "Disaster Falls." The memories flooded her mind. Thrashing, kicking, trying desperately to break free. Her lungs on fire, Brianna longed for fresh air. The rest was hidden in her subconscious. The only other memories were seeing Nate and gasping for air. *Is there any way out of this predicament? Where is the life jacket this time?*

"I need some time to process," Brianna said, her mind still reeling from the adrenalin flow of the recollection.

"You have one week," snapped Batten. "We'll meet in my office next Monday for lunch. If you're not up for this, we'll find someone else who is." He was already flipping through his mental address list of young leaders who could take Brianna's place. *Silly girl. Doesn't she realize how easily she too can be outsourced? I've got a company to reorganize, and no one is going to stand in my way. If I play my cards right, maybe the search for a new CEO will stop right at this desk.*

"All right," replied Brianna. "I'll have an answer for you by next Monday."

As she stood up to leave, only one question floated to the surface of her mind. *What am I going to say to the team this afternoon?*

What is a leadership style? In an article published in the *Harvard Business Review*, Daniel Goleman defined leadership styles as distinctive or characteristic modes of leadership, such as coercive, authoritative, affiliative, democratic, pacesetting, or coaching.[1] The acting CEO of Handover, Daniel Batten, is leading from a very authoritative style. In fact, his style is also coercive. It's his way or the highway, and he has an ulterior motive. Brianna is thinking about team leadership, a much more collaborative or democratic style. Hierarchy and collaboration, of course, are the extreme ends of the spectrum, and many other expressions of leadership style exist. However, what does research reveal about the leadership preferences in the various generations?

The particular leadership styles that characterized the mid-1900s, the time when the Silent Generation began giving leadership to new organizations, advocated a top-down approach. The world had just come through the Second World War. Military leadership had dominated, and those in the Silent Generation were their protégés. Clear vision and direction propelled decisive leadership decisions. Command and control was the leadership style of the day.

By the 1960s, however, vast social change was sweeping

through the United States. Authority figures were being challenged. The command-and-control model was losing its grip. One executive Boomer who served in the Vietnam War described this shift:

> When it came to my generation, because of the failure of vision in the Vietnam War, the only way they could keep people was to only keep them there for 365 days. That is what we had instead of leadership; a very limited commitment . . . a bridging between the total loyalty of the Builder Generation because of the clear moral vision of WWII and the very limited loyalty and rebellion almost of my generation. I think that paved the way to the almost total lack of loyalty among postmoderns to a bigger organization. In that scenario, loyalty to relationships takes the place of loyalty to an organization. There can be loyalty to a vision but not to an organization.[2]

As mentioned in the last chapter, older Boomers like Daniel Batten often reflect the same leadership patterns as the Silent Generation, but younger Boomers prefer a more collaborative, consensus style of leadership. For Gen Xers and Millennials, there is no question. Collaboration is foremost, reflecting their desire for relationship, feedback, mentoring, and day-to-day focus.[3]

In my research study on leadership transition and generations, all cohorts were asked to describe their leadership style. Although hierarchical styles of leadership were represented in each generational cohort (depending on cultural representation), the results indicated a continuum of change, moving from more strongly hierarchical to collaborative as one moves from the Silent Generation to Generation X.[4] The Millennials are even more specific. They are looking for leaders who are dedicated, creative, and focused and who care about them personally.[5]

Leaders in the Silent cohort and older Boomers tended to describe their leadership style with words like *strong, up-front, confrontive, efficient, and task-oriented.* However, even they recognize the shift that is taking place. Another executive Boomer had this to say:

> When I began I was incredibly directive and had an unbelievable sense of where we were supposed to go. . . . That probably dominated the first twenty years of my leadership, and when you are dealing with young people who don't know what they are doing, it is actually pretty effective. But when I started getting people who were very qualified in their own areas, I went through a major crisis and retooling, because the directive style actually discouraged them in their development. . . . I became far more team oriented and more of a coach. . . . That approach . . . is the only thing that is really usable at this stage.[6]

In my research, a majority of younger Boomers and Gen Xers described themselves as nondirective, using words like *inclusive, consensus, team player, and relationship-oriented.* When discussing their leadership behaviors, they talked about "coming alongside," "being transparent," "caring," "releasing," "being genuine," "creating space," "being hands-off," "coaching," and "being a learning leader." Listen to some of the comments from leaders in the Gen X cohort (names have been changed):

- "I am more of a coach. . . . My style is more inclusive, allowing people to come to a conclusion." —James, age thirty-three
- "I am inclusive in my decision making, so I will draw on the group. It is important to me that people are included in the decision-making process, because they will have to own that decision as well." —Alison, age twenty-eight
- "I am very much a team player, deliberately working to include people. I want to see the person and build relationship." —Mike, age thirty-three
- "We have the oldies, and they are the pioneers and visionaries. That is one leadership style, and that is top-down. I'm sure they want to be more inclusive, but they are used to their own style." —Carla, age thirty-three
- "Before I make decisions, I always confer with other leaders so that I have a good communication with them. It is important to me to have consensus with at least three to five other people." —Joseph, age thirty[7]

Once again, the Millennials are even more distanced from command and control. In a 2007 article in *Fortune* magazine, this cohort is described as ambitious, demanding, and questioning of everything. The article went on to describe a twenty-two-year-old accountant who negotiated with his firm to move him to his chosen city as well as to allow him to arrange his schedule to train for a bodybuilding competition. The young man had this to say about the company: "You know what? This firm has shown a commitment to me. Let me in turn show some commitment to the firm. So this is a merger, if you will—Josh and KPMG."

Wrap your corporate head around that one! What kind of leadership style will Josh have? That is still to be seen, but he may not be at KPMG when his opportunity for leadership comes knocking. He chose accounting so that he could have "transferable skills."[8]

Of course, additional dynamics, such as personality, culture, gender, and organizational ethos, also factor into leadership style. Nevertheless, it is clear that there has been a shift away from command and control to more of a consensus-building style of leadership. Will this trend last? Time will tell. One thing, however, is sure. If you want to keep younger employees, compromises will need to be made. And most of those adjustments will probably come from your side. You might be able to outsource their work, but they may not stick around long enough to give you the chance.

The clock was ticking. Brad, George, and Nate would be coming at 3:00 P.M. Brianna had a plan, but it would require trust, loyalty, and teamwork. *Will they go for it? I guess I'll see if the rafting trip really did bond us together. I hope so.*

George was knocking on the door. Nate and Brad were right behind him.

"Come on in, guys," said Brianna. "Have I got some news for you."

CHAPTER EIGHT

Lost Paddle

Who Wants to Be a Leader?

"Take a seat, fellas. And close the door behind you—securely," said Brianna with a hushed, but commanding, voice. She had their attention immediately.

"What happened?" asked Nate. He loved suspense.

"Brad, you were right," Brianna declared. "Batten is all about downsizing. I don't know why, since he is only the interim CEO, but he seems hell-bent on making changes before the new person is appointed."

Brad's face was already turning red again. Brianna stopped him in his tracks. "Wait, Brad. Before you go off again, listen to me. I have a plan," she whispered.

Three pairs of eyes stared in her direction.

"George, you have always declared your trust in Edward White—that he would do the right thing. Do you still believe that?" Brianna asked.

"Absolutely," replied George. "No hesitation whatsoever. Why?"

"I want us to develop a counterproposal for our department and go directly to White. Let's appeal what Batten is suggesting," exclaimed Brianna. "But this will take real teamwork, confidentiality, and trust. If we're not successful, we will probably all lose our jobs. But if we are heard and White agrees, we might all win and get the new CEO faster."

The three men sat in silence, absorbing Brianna's words.

Brad was the first to speak up. "I want to know what's at stake here, Brianna. What exactly is Batten proposing?"

"He wants to outsource software design and computer systems maintenance," responded Brianna with a clarity and confidence that surprised her. "I protested, and he gave me one week to decide whether or not I'll lead that initiative."

Suddenly memories of "Lost Paddle" came flooding back into Brad's mind. *She saved my backside in that rapid. Now she is willing to do it again. There is more to this chick than I ever imagined.*

"Brianna, I owe you an apology," Brad confessed. "I've resented you. And I really went off on you this morning. I'm sorry." His voice was as subdued as a peaceful patch of water between rapids.

"Thanks, Brad," replied Brianna. "That means a lot to me."

"Okay guys, what do you think?" Brianna asked. "To navigate this challenge, we need all paddles pulling in the same direction. Are you with me?"

"I guess I've got nothing to lose," said George. "I really want to keep working."

"I'm in," declared Nate.

"Glad to hear it, Nate," responded Brianna with a grin. "Batten said that you and I are the new leaders. I think he's going to be surprised."

"Brad and George, I'd like you to prepare a detailed list of what you do, and get it to me by tomorrow noon," Brianna directed.

"Nate, you and I need to start doing our homework to put together a counterproposal. Let's begin first thing tomorrow morning."

What a Monday this had been! The foursome left the office, got in their cars, and headed for home, each lost in his or her own thoughts. Two of them, however, were experiencing almost identical reservations. Both Nate and Brianna were pummeled with thoughts as strong as the crashing waters of "Disaster Falls." *What have I gotten myself into? Do I really want to be a leader? What is this going to cost me?*

They both hit the Internet right after dinner and began to work.

Who aspires to be a leader? Interesting question. Daniel

Batten, an older Boomer, wants to be the new CEO. But he won't come out and say it. He plans to demonstrate his competencies in the hope that the pendulum swings in his direction. Edward C. White, the founder, is a solid member of the Silent Generation and has carried leadership his entire life. Reluctantly, he sees the need to step aside. Brad, a younger Boomer, feels skipped over. He is too young to retire but too old for key leadership—the Boomer nightmare. Brianna, a Gen Xer, and Nate, a Millennial, have been recognized as up-and-coming leaders. But they aren't even sure that's what they want.

Welcome to the multigenerational workplace.

How does each of these four unique generations perceive leadership? Leaders from the Silent Generation rarely use emotive words to describe leadership. They talk about duty and getting things done. Older Boomers like Daniel Batten are similar. A high degree of responsibility drives them. They don't give up easily.

One Boomer captured it this way: "I did not face a war, did not have to fight, no draft, etc. War and depression created that sense of responsibility [for my father's generation]. For me, Desert Storm was the first I knew of any wars."[1]

These Boomers want to stay in the workforce, however, and are not giving up leadership easily. They may not feel as compelled by responsibility as the older members of their cohort; but a drive to achieve and climb the corporate ladder is still alive and well.

My research indicates that the younger Boomers may be more concerned with issues of infrastructure and team leadership.[2] They describe themselves as relational, inclusive, collaborative, managing, trainers and equippers, quiet, controlling, task-oriented, and highly productive. An older Boomer executive remarked, "If you are talking forty-five or under, you are talking about nondirective, team-oriented, process-oriented, collaborative, wanting to be human in the process. But I still see highly productive, highly task-oriented people."[3]

However, many of these younger Boomers perceive themselves as a skipped-over generation of leadership. One Boomer leader lamented:

> At times it seems as if the older generation is moving towards the younger one and almost skipping a generation, skipping my generation. And yet we are the ones who will take things forward to the next stage. We must not miss out on the middle group, because we will lose a lot of our new up-and-coming senior leaders. . . . We will lose the wisdom of the future. We have the wisdom right now, but [the older generation is] going to die out. And so we need the people who will father and mother these younger leaders coming up; and if we lose the middle group, we lose the whole thing.[4]

A noteworthy change begins to appear among Gen X leaders. Although some will still use words like *responsibility* and *commitment*, a majority of these younger leaders use much more emotive terms, such as "scary," "lots of criticism," "passion," "revolution," "impatience," "unsatisfied," "cautious," "nervous," "fear," "excited," "lonely," "isolated," "frustrated," "hopelessness," "struggling," and "feeling abandoned." While a couple of these terms reveal positive emotions, most of them are negative. The following quotes from Gen Xers in leadership provide more insight (names have been changed):

- "I'm not sure I want to be a leader. . . . Leadership is a lot of responsibility, a lot of hard work, perhaps a lot of criticism." —Mary, age thirty-five
- "A lot of my generation wants to move closer to leadership because it creates space. I've got my vision, I've got my dream, and in some odd way, I'm going to need leadership for permission, a platform, or teaching." —Donna, age thirty
- "I hear responsibility, less freedom, being tied down, being accountable, a bit scary." —Tina, age thirty-three
- "We are visionary but also struggle with hopelessness." —David, age thirty-one
- "There is a hunger for the truth, and we do not want to accept the status quo; we want to know why we are doing what we are doing." —George, age twenty-eight
- "Young people uprising, passionate, outspoken, but perhaps that was every generation. Wanting to take an issue by the horns and run with it. *Passionate* would sum it up. There is also a nervousness—Can I really do that?" —Jake, age twenty-seven[5]

Ironically, all of these respondents are in leadership roles, which raises a vital question. If duty and loyalty are not the driving factors for younger leaders, what keeps them in leadership roles in spite of these painful emotions?

Overall, Gen X leaders seem open to more leadership but are cautious and delineate specific conditions for assuming additional responsibility.[6] Many Gen Xers are opting to start their own companies, willing to take risks and carry a heavy load in order to be in charge of their own lives and schedules.[7]

Millennials desire training and a gradual handing over of responsibility. The issue of commitment hits a definite nerve among this cohort. In a focus group meeting, I asked some Millennials how they would feel about making a two-year commitment. The immediate response was "scared to death." They went on to say that they would "feel trapped, because we want to try different things. We like freedom and not being tied down." This cohort can be ambivalent about leadership. As one Millennial put it, "Either you don't care or you really want it because it gives you status."[8]

The next decade will reveal the leadership preferences and capacities of this generation.

Nate and Brianna had been sending instant messages back and forth all evening. Nate had been looking into alternatives to outsourcing. Brianna had contacted a few headhunters, trolling for possible candidates to suggest to Edward C. White. Although she felt guilty doing it, she wondered if Daniel Batten was really looking for a new CEO. She couldn't take a chance.

They had only a few days to come up with a realistic counterproposal. The challenge reminded her of the "Bus Stop." If they couldn't navigate around this situation, they would be at the mercy of the organizational whirlpool, and some people were going to get tossed out of the boat. As Brianna drifted off to sleep, she remembered what she had yelled in the turbulence of that rapid: "We can do it!" *I sure hope so.*

CHAPTER NINE

Bus Stop

Balancing Task and Relationship

Waking long before dawn, Brianna felt the warm little body of Abby cuddled next to her. The little angel had crept in at some point during the night. Her husband, Kyle, was sleeping peacefully on the opposite side of Brianna. In her semi-awake, relaxed state, the compelling question from the day before floated back to the surface of her mind: Do I really want to be a leader? *Too late now, girl. You already are.*

Rolling quietly out of bed, Brianna headed to the computer, woke it up, and pressed the Send/Receive button. E-mails began streaming onto the screen. One of them caught her attention immediately. The subject line was "Potential CEO." One of the headhunters had already responded. Adrenalin began to flow as it had when she first saw the "Bus Stop." As she clicked to open the message, another twinge of guilt struck her. "Delete" was always an option. *There's no turning back now. You have to paddle around this situation.* Brianna began to read the short e-mail:

> I've got just the guy for Handover. Peter Durham is in his early forties, highly qualified to lead a mid-sized company, and full of energy. He is innovative, likes to work as a team, and I think he could really move things forward. A number of companies are considering him for CEO. His credentials are impeccable. If you're interested, give me a call.

Brianna wasted no time. Even though she knew there was no way that Nate would be up at this hour, she called him. *The cost of leadership.* A slight smile formed on her lips. *Get up, Dude.*

An irritating, persistent tone pierced Nate's subconscious. *What the . . . ? Who could be calling me this early? And where is the phone?* Stumbling across the bedroom, Nate found his cell phone underneath a pair of jeans. It was still ringing. Brianna's number glared at him on the screen.

"Hello. This better be good."

"Nate, I'm really sorry," gushed Brianna. "But I've just heard back from one of the headhunters. It looks promising."

"Serious?" Nate was wide awake now. "Read it to me."

One minute later he had already forgiven Brianna for the rude awakening.

"Brianna, that's awesome. What do we do now?"

"We don't have much time," Brianna replied. "Let's meet at the office in an hour and discuss our next step. I'll grab some breakfast on the way."

"Sounds good. I'll meet you there," said Nate.

"And Nate, one more thing. I think it's going to be a long day. Prepare to stay late, okay?"

"Whatever," quipped Nate. *How late is "late?" I've got a life, you know.*

Brianna showered, dressed, and woke Kyle with a kiss. "Honey, I need to go into the office early. Can you take Abby to preschool this morning?"

"Okay, sure," Kyle replied, still groggy.

"Oh, and one more thing," continued Brianna. "I don't know how late I'll have to work today. Something urgent just came up. Can you pick Abby up and take care of dinner too?"

"Brianna, what is going on?" snapped Kyle, suddenly awake and very aware of the conversation. "I know you've been appointed project leader, but does that mean you don't have a life anymore?"

"Honey, it's only for a few days. This is a really stressful week. Please cut me some slack. I promise this won't be a trend."

"Okay," Kyle replied, grudgingly. "Just remember you have two other people in your life."

"How could I ever forget that?" Brianna responded with a smile, as she planted a kiss on Abby's forehead and another one on his. "See you later."

As Brianna drove to the office a whirlpool of thoughts swirled through her mind. *Is this what leadership requires? If Daniel Batten finds out that I contacted a headhunter, I'm dead in the water. I can't afford to lose my job. Oh come on; you can get another job. Get to Edward C. White fast. I hope Nate is willing to work as hard as I am. I wonder if Abby is up yet.*

"Stop it!" Brianna yelled at herself, glancing in the rearview mirror to see if anyone had seen her reprimand herself. *Just get to work and deal with it.* She took a slight detour to pick up a cappuccino at Starbucks.

Thirty minutes later she and Nate had come up with a plan of action. The first step was to inform George and Brad. The counterproposal was essential. And then the package would be complete: a viable candidate for CEO and a plea to keep the IT department intact until a new CEO took over. It was going to be a long day.

Balancing task and relationship was not a hot topic for the Silent Generation. On the home front, a majority of women stayed at home and kept things together. Men went to work to accomplish the task; hopefully there was enough time left over for real relationship when they got home. On the job, work and time were clearly preeminent when compared to relationship.

As one executive in the Silent cohort remarked in the course of my research, "Work and time [are] always most important. Relationships come third."[1] Another leader commented concisely, "Relationships are secondary; you deal with them if they are inhibitive."[2] However, a third executive in the same cohort expressed a frustration that, in his opinion, many leaders in the Silent Generation feel:

> Leaders in my generation view this [tension between work and time and relationship] with a great deal of frustration, as I see it. The pressures of modernity continually influence us toward value and identity being in better and more-perfected performance. Relationships are a means to this end and more or less cease when the end comes. Time is of the essence, and so relationships of the deeper-heart kind are minimal or nonexistent for the most part.[3]

Among the first-wave Boomers, a similar emphasis on work or task was also conveyed. Some respondents in this group, however, identified a shift toward the relational in the Boomer generation. An executive in this older Boomer category commented: "The Boomer generation, in my estimation, turned things around relationally. Think of the hippies and the communes, community. . . . Relationships became more important than task and time. This shift was a watershed in our society, and I became an adult as that was happening, ushering me into making relationship a priority over task and time."[4]

Other first-wave Boomers have observed a change in priorities as this cohort has become older. One leader captured it well: "My generation is seeing that time is going a lot more quickly than it used to. Therefore, we are becoming more aware of quality of relationships and trimming down our involvement so that we can give ourselves to something, so we can really make a difference in relationships that are important to us."[5]

In my research, leaders who would be characterized as second-wave Boomers indicated a continued emphasis on work and time as opposed to relationship. However, several were quite vocal about the unhealthiness of this (names have been changed):

- "Time is very important, it is short, we are the Baby Boomers, now make it happen. Task is very important, and relationship would come second. And I battle with this tension, because sometimes I think we lean too much toward relationship. Sometimes there are just tasks that need to be done. So let's do the task and build relationship as we work. Work ethic is very important to me." —Norm, age forty-five
- "Very unhealthy. There are a number of us who are really taking stock now: The adrenalin of the twenties and thirties is gone, and now where is my greatest contribution going to be? That is a central question. I've seen a lot of workaholics in my generation because there are a lot of perfectionists—get the work done, diligence—the discipline is there in our generation to just get your head down and get on with it. But I

think that has been to our detriment." —Cathy, age forty-five

- "Typically the individualist Protestant work ethic has dominated—work hard, use any time wisely, and make work more important than relationships. What a killer. I have been learning a different way from my non-Western and twenty-something friends." —Jay, age forty-five[6]

Comments from older Gen X leaders still reflect an emphasis on task, but the shift toward relationship is complete in the younger ones. Notice the progression in the following comments (names have been changed):

- "I am very work oriented, but at the same time I am very relational. If I want to get a job done and it involves people, I cannot go forward without relationships. I think that is typical of my generation." —Vicki, age thirty-five
- "I think my generation is still working hard to accomplish something." —Lisa, age forty-one
- "I have a tendency to work a lot. And I realize that those around me have a tendency to work a lot. That puts relationships in the background." —Preston, age forty
- "Between twenty and thirty, I think we are considered to be in the same generation, but there is quite a gap. I think the thirties are more linked to the Boomer

generation, and the younger ones in the twenties are more linked to the Gen Xers. I think the Boomers are more work oriented, but the younger people are more relational." —Scott, age thirty-one

- "In general, I think my generation, Gen X, tends to be more task-oriented at the top end of the generation, but in the middle and lower brackets we tend to be relationship-oriented, personal-time-oriented, and less task-oriented." —Jerry, age thirty-two
- "I think in my generation there is a value on relationships and maybe less a value for just the work. . . . I see in the generation before me, the Boomers, much more of a 'head to the grindstone' attitude, push through it. My generation is resistant to that; let's try another way, or just watch some TV for a while, or joke about this. There is a softer, less disciplined approach in general." —Tommy, age thirty-three
- "Time is a little more loose, and relationship takes a little bit higher of a priority as compared to before. . . . People will show up late for work, but they still want to know they are your buddy. As long as the job gets done, who cares how long it takes? . . . I think it is a lot more based on relationship, time is more loose, task gets done." —Ray, age twenty-eight[7]

One Gen Xer in his late twenties described this task-relationship balance and its connection to home life quite poignantly:

> I think our generation is more relational than previous generations. . . . I think we are still learning what that means, coming into leadership and taking on positions of responsibility where there is more to do than there is time. How do I cope with that? How do I cope with the to-do list that will never get done? If I don't make time for the family, I'm dying on the inside. If I don't make time for beauty, for example, sport, allowing for creativity, I'm dying as well. So I'm never going to be prepared to be in the office all day, every day. I'm never going to go there in the way that other generations would put that as an absolute value.[8]

Research supports this changing dynamic, especially with respect to personal life and the balance between work and home. As mentioned earlier in the book, the social milieu of the Gen X cohort was characterized by divorce, broken homes, latchkey kids, pop culture, and the growing influence of the media. Studies cite more depression and emotional problems within this generational grouping, combined with a deep loneliness that fosters a yearning for relationships and community. For these Gen X leaders, relationship definitely takes priority over task.[9]

For the Millennials, this is a no-brainer. Relationships rule. In a *Fortune* magazine article entitled "Attracting the Twentysomething Worker," the author writes, "If there isn't a good reason for that long commute or late night, don't expect them to do it. When it comes to loyalty, the companies they work for are last on their list—behind their families, their friends, their communities, their co-workers and, of course, themselves."[10] Task is definitely not the driving force in this generational cohort.

Nate met Brad in the parking lot. "Dude, Brianna needs you in her office ASAP. We've got some good news."

"What's up?" Brad asked. *Can these two really pull this off?*

"I don't want to spoil it," Nate replied. "But we've got a lot of work to do. Let's go!" Nate walked with him to Brianna's office, where George was already seated.

"Morning, guys," began Brianna. "I've heard back from one of the headhunters. We've got a good prospect for Mr. White to consider. His name is Peter Durham."

Nate dove into the conversation. "I've already Googled this guy. He sounds awesome. Incredible experience. Durham is currently available but not for long. Evidently a number of companies are after him."

"What are we going to do?" asked George, still stunned by all of the new developments of the past week.

"I'm going to go directly to Edward C. White and submit Durham's name, along with our counterproposal to keep this department intact until a new CEO takes over," replied Brianna.

"You go, girl!" Brad quipped.

A nervous laugh emerged from Brianna, revealing a mixture

of satisfaction and stress. "So are we together on this?" she inquired, sounding out the group. "If not, I won't do it."

Three male heads nodded in agreement.

"George and Brad, remember that I need your job description lists today by noon. We don't have much time."

"And Nate, please e-mail Mr. White's executive assistant to see if I can get an appointment with him this week. The sooner the better."

"Aye, aye," joked Nate. "You're starting to sound like our rafting guide, Daniella." He stood up and mimicked Daniella pulling out the six-inch hunting knife. "One final thing," he said in an exaggerated Swiss-German accent. "Any questions?"

The one-liner elicited uproarious laughter from all four of them. Each one had vivid memories of Daniella, that knife, and the rafting trip that had knit them together.

A few hours later Brianna had all that she needed to proceed. Edward C. White would meet with her Thursday at 10:00 A.M. The job descriptions for Brad and George were on her desk.

She had less than forty-eight hours to prepare the counterproposal and work up the nerve to present it. The "Bus Stop" was staring her in the face once again. *It's all or nothing. Come on, girl; paddle for all you're worth.*

CHAPTER TEN

Table Saw

Character of a Leader

Typing furiously on her keyboard, Brianna kept an eye on the clock. She wanted to try to make it home in time to share dinner with Abby and her man.

A knock on the door startled her.

"Come in," said Brianna.

Daniel Batten strolled into her office. "Got a minute?" he asked.

Brianna froze. "Uh, sure," she replied, trying to regain her composure. *Has he heard something?*

Batten's eyes bored a hole into her. "What are you working on so studiously?" he inquired. "Have you given any more thought about our little meeting?"

Hesitating only a second, Brianna got her mental act together. "George and Brad have given me their job descriptions. I have a bigger picture of what they actually do. I'll have an answer for you by next Monday."

"Why do you need their job descriptions?" Batten demanded. "Their work is going to be outsourced." His casual "drop-by-the-office" demeanor changed in an instant. *This woman doesn't know who she's dealing with.*

"Look, I'm trying to finish up some work so that I can get home for dinner," replied Brianna. "I'll see you Monday at noon." *This guy is a real jerk. On a scale of one to ten for character, he gets a minus one.*

"Don't be late," commanded Batten. He whipped around and was out the door.

A cold sweat broke out on Brianna. *What kind of company will Handover become if he is the next CEO?* That simple thought renewed her energy as she resumed typing and glanced at the clock. *Okay, so I skip a meal. It won't hurt me.*

Three hours later she returned home, finding Abby already asleep and a sullen husband on the sofa. *I have no energy to deal with this.* She washed her face, brushed her teeth, and climbed into bed. The next thing she knew, it was morning.

The next day was a blur. Brianna arrived at the office by nine, met with George, Nate, and Brad for several hours to refine the counterproposal, and talked on the phone with the headhunter. "Please tell Peter Durham that we are going to submit his name for consideration," she said. *This feels so surreal. I just want to get this whole thing behind me.*

Thursday morning finally arrived, and Brianna was standing in front of Edward C. White's door at 9:55 A.M. She breathed deeply and knocked on the door.

"Come in," responded a deep baritone voice.

Brianna walked in, trying to hold her head high, file folder tucked under her arm. She had worn high heels to compensate for her stature. "Mr. White, thank you for taking the time to see me," Brianna began. "I know you must be really busy with the company transition."

"Brianna, have a seat. What can I do for you? You work in the IT department, correct?" His voice seemed like that of a father's—steady but gentle.

"Yes sir," she replied. "I've been with Handover for five years. I design webpages."

"Oh, yes!" exclaimed the founder. "Your work is excellent. Very creative. Now, what brings you to my office today?"

Brianna took a deep breath and looked directly at him. "Sir, I have a few concerns about the transition." Suddenly, her words gushed out like a waterfall. She talked about their rafting trip. She told him all about Batten's plans to outsource work from IT and to let George, and most likely Brad go. She dropped the name of Peter Durham as a potential candidate for CEO. Suddenly, like a rapid that had run its course, Brianna was done. She didn't know what would happen, but she felt at peace.

"Well," began Edward C. White, "this is highly unusual. Why haven't you gone to Daniel Batten with all of this? That would be the normal procedure. Chain of command, you know."

"To be quite frank, sir, I'm not sure he really wants to find another CEO."

"Are you implying that he wants the job?"

"Yes," replied Brianna. "Why make such sweeping changes before a new CEO comes on board?"

"You have a point," White said. "Okay, give me the number for Peter Durham, and I'll call him myself. In the meantime, keep this to yourself."

"Thank you!" exclaimed Brianna. She stood up and left his office. Once out the door, she almost collapsed.

Instead of meeting with Daniel Batten on Monday, Brianna was sitting in a department leaders' meeting, listening to Edward C. White announce his intention to pursue a Mr. Peter Durham as potential CEO of Handover. Meanwhile, Daniel Batten was on a flight back to the West Coast. The last communication she received from him was via e-mail, and it was ugly. But it was over. *Thank goodness he's gone. That's one person out of the raft that I don't mind losing.*

Six weeks later it was a done deal. Durham was the new CEO, and people were excited. There had been a number of company-wide staff meetings, and he was impressive. Durham was not a company insider. His ideas, especially on leadership, were fresh and innovative. He wanted a more collaborative leadership style. Durham exuded warmth and had obviously convinced Edward C. White of his ability to lead the company into the future.

George, Brad, Brianna, and Nate were pleased and eager to work with the new CEO. Of course, they also had questions. Once the calm waters passed, what kind of person would he really be? How would he navigate the rapids of global competition and corporate pressure? Did he truly have integrity?

Although they had not paddled through "Table Saw," the final rapid planned for their team-building experience, Nate had showed it to them on the GPS software. It could rip a raft into shreds. Did Peter Durham have the character needed to lead Handover? They would soon see.

How does character factor into leadership? Does it matter? George trusts Edward White, commenting often about his integrity. Brianna suspected that Daniel Batten had ulterior motives, and she was proved correct. When those motives were revealed, his true character came out. Brad wonders about Peter Durham's moral fiber and whether he has what it takes to lead the company.

General H. Norman Schwarzkopf said, "Leadership is a combination of strategy and character. If you must be without one, be without the strategy." Business leaders agree. In the introduction to his book, *The 21 Indispensable Qualities of a Leader*, John Maxwell poses a compelling question: "What makes people want to follow a leader?" His conclusion? "The answer lies in the character qualities of the individual person." Maxwell's premise is that leadership develops from the inside out.[1]

Various definitions of leadership have evolved over the span of the four generations currently in the workforce. Prior to 1950, leadership theory focused almost solely on the traits of the leader, presupposing that some people were born with outstanding competencies that qualified them for leadership.[2] This type of thinking was often referred to as the "great man theory."[3]

Another leader-centered approach was the charismatic profile, with an emphasis on extraordinary qualities and high levels of vision, charisma, conviction, self-confidence, and determination.[4] However, Peter Drucker certainly put this concept into perspective with his comment, "Charisma becomes the undoing of leaders. It makes them inflexible, convinced of their own infallibility, unable to change."[5]

Leadership theorists gradually began moving away from an emphasis on traits and began to examine behaviors. Next came an emphasis on management, and the term "transactional leadership" came into being.[6] By the 1990s interest shifted away from an emphasis on the leader to a greater attention on the followers, as the concept of "transformational leadership" emerged. The research supporting this theory rejects the notion that leaders are born. On the contrary, everyone has the capacity for leadership, which needs to be developed over time.[7]

Within the last few years, the concept of "emotional intelligence" and leadership has been the rave. Daniel Goleman's book, *Primal Leadership: Learning to Lead with Emotional Intelligence*, insists that the primary job of leadership is emotional, and those leaders with a higher emotional intelligence will be more successful. What is emotional intelligence? Goleman defines it as a set of skills such as impulse control, self-motivation, empathy, and social competence.[8] Sounds a lot like character, doesn't it?

So leadership theory has moved from the "great man theory" to personal character. As Brad might say, "We've come a long way, baby." In what ways does each generation view character in leaders?

For the Silent Generation, those committed to duty and responsibility, character revolves around integrity, faithfulness, self-control, and foresight. During my research, an executive in this cohort made this comment about character: "Integrity and keeping your word. Everything either falls or rises on keeping your word."[9] Another senior executive focused his remarks on foresight, defining it as "really understanding when you make a decision what the implications might be for a year, five years, ten years down the road. And it is one of the major failures of leaders, that they do not have foresight."[10]

In a large empirical study, *credibility* ranked second, behind *listens well*, among the top twelve characteristics of leaders identified by the Silent, or Mature, Generation.[11] Interestingly, credibility ranked number one among the Boomers and Gen Xers in the same study.[12] Credibility is a major character requirement for the Boomers.

Foresight was also mentioned during my research. One Boomer remarked that leaders "have to be able to see where they are going, what their direction is. They almost have to see the end product in their heart, not with all the end pieces, but they have to be able to see a direction or they cannot lead anyone to it."[13]

Once again, the Gen X cohort had some interesting things to say about character and leadership. The characteristics they emphasized were caring concern, encouragement, love, humility, servanthood, teachability, and integrity. A particular emphasis on integrity was found especially among those in the second half of the cohort (names have been changed):

- "Integrity. Being a person who lives out what you say; someone you can trust and believe in. Being a person of your word; living out who I am in every area, not just in the classroom but also in private, in social times. Being somebody who can be trusted with a confidence; being loyal to people." —Susan, age twenty-eight
- "Integrity about what you do; your word carries authority because you are going to do what you said you would do. But integrity spills over into a bunch of different areas of management, including the management of your personal life. People maintaining true to their values." —John, age twenty-eight
- "Integrity, someone who actually demonstrates what they say or do." —Peter, age twenty-seven
- "Integrity. Don't say anything you won't do; don't do anything that you don't want reproduced. How do you live your life when no one is looking?" —Rob, age thirty-two[14]

Caring concern highlights characteristics like encouragement, dependability, and spending time together, both inside and outside of the business setting. As one Gen X leader expressed it, "A leader has a lot to do with a father; has an ability in some ways to go beforehand, but also to raise up, to draw out, to encourage. . . . In a practical way, that would mean I show my care; it is visible, not just verbal; it is visible in my actions; I look after the ones I lead; I care about their well-being."[15]

In a large empirical study, this cohort also expressed a desire for clear focus and wants leaders who will encourage, recognize contributions, and give feedback.[16]

The Millennial cohort was the only group in the empirical study that did not mention *credibility* in the top twelve leadership descriptions. Their top choice was *dedicated*. These youngest members of the workforce prefer leaders who are dedicated but who also care about them personally.[17] In a focus group meeting of young Millennials, one person captured it succinctly: "No one in our generation wants to be told what to do. We respond better to relationship. Less fear-based. Heavy influence."[18]

The bottom line is that character does matter in leadership. It always has, and it always will. Indeed, character is becoming even more critical. Younger leaders no longer automatically ascribe respect to those who lead them; it must be earned. And the preferred currency is character.

Enjoying a Friday midmorning break with bagels and coffee, the IT foursome gathered in Brianna's office.

"Hey, Brianna, are you still our boss?" quipped Nate.

"No idea," Brianna replied with a chuckle. "Everything is up in the air at this point. I'm just glad that Batten is back on the West Coast, and George and Brad still have their jobs."

"Amen to that!" exclaimed George.

Someone rapped at the door.

"Enter at your own risk," Brad declared with a smile. *The weekend is almost here. Time to relax.*

Peter Durham strolled in. "Is this the IT group that I've heard so much about?" A wry smile crossed his lips. "I hear that you all had something to do with my getting this job."

They almost lost their bagels.

"That's us," responded Nate with a grin. "IT stands for 'instant trouble.'"

Brad shot him a look of disbelief.

Durham laughed out loud. "I like a sense of humor."

"I just dropped by to say that I look forward to getting to know each one of you. Brianna, I'd like you to remain department leader for the time being. I'll meet with all department heads on Monday at 9:00 A.M. okay?"

She nodded her affirmation.

"See you then," said Durham. "Have a good weekend, everyone."

He turned and left the office.

A similar thought swam through each of their heads. *So far, so good.*

CHAPTER ELEVEN

Handing Over the Rudder

Letting Go of Control

A wide, substantial, but blank whiteboard greeted Brianna and the other department leaders as they filed into the conference room on Monday morning to meet with the new CEO. Each one received a whiteboard marker as he or she entered. The group numbered around thirty.

Lining the walls were tables filled with fresh fruit, bottled water, scones of all types, cream cheese, butter, jam, and, of course, carafes of coffee, tea, and ice water. One important item was missing, however—chairs. There was not one single chair in the room.

At promptly 9:00 A.M. Peter Durham strode into the room,

walking right into the middle of the group. "Good morning, folks," he boomed. "Great to see each one of you." He didn't seem to notice that the chairs were missing.

"We're going to start this morning by dividing into two groups." He quickly called out the names. "You may have noticed the lack of chairs in here," stated Durham.

"That's an understatement," quipped one of the department heads.

A broad smile cracked Durham's handsome face.

"I want each person in Group One to go into the adjoining room, get a chair, bring it in here, and pull off the name of the person from Group Two that is taped underneath the seat. Find that person, and interview them. I want to know where they are from, a little family biography, where they studied, what attracted them to Handover, how long they've worked here, and which department they work in. Questions, anyone?"

"Okay, you have ten minutes. Go!"

The room came alive with fifteen interviews happening simultaneously while Durham looked on. At the end of ten minutes, he asked the pairs to switch roles. As the whole group was called back together, there was a noticeable difference in the room. People were beginning to relax. An air of expectancy filled the place like football fans waiting for their team to take the field.

Next they were placed in groups with people from different departments and asked two simple questions: *In ten years, what do you see Handover doing? And how do we get there?* Vigorous discussions ensued. Brianna glanced up and took a quick survey around the room. What she observed energized her—diverse personalities, men and women, younger and older. Each one with a strategic role but normally segmented by department and not able to create this kind of synergy. *Wow!*

Peter Durham facilitated the feedback from the groups, making copious notes on the whiteboard for all to see. He, too, was clearly invigorated by the process. After each group had reported, Durham stepped back from the board and surveyed the thirty managers in front of him—some sitting, some standing. They still had only fifteen chairs in the room.

"Folks, do you see the possibilities here? This company has a solid underpinning, strong financials, and tremendous potential. However, we cannot just kick back and float along. Globalization is creating enormous pressure—as well as fantastic opportunities. We have to work together as a team to navigate these new rapids." He glanced over at Brianna and winked. *Ohmigosh—he knows about the rafting trip!*

Durham stepped dramatically to the whiteboard and erased it. "Great vision, but now we need to consider our everyday realities. I want each department represented on this board with the names of your staff, your current challenges, and proposed solutions." Four people rushed to the board and began the process. Peter Durham grabbed a chair and started taking notes. Within thirty minutes, every department was represented on the whiteboard. It was a sight to behold.

"Okay, let's come back together," said Durham. "Everyone please join me here at the whiteboard." The group formed a semicircle, facing Peter Durham. "Thank you for your participation today. Each one of you is vital to our forward movement as a company. We will be meeting every Monday morning to collaborate, review progress, and work through challenges. Next week we'll begin by reviewing the input you've given me today. Any questions?"

A few hands went up. "Is Mr. White stepping aside completely and giving you free reign with the company?" "What happens with the current board of directors?" "Will there be any kind of special ceremony to honor the founder?"

"You read my thoughts," joked Durham. "Those items were next on the agenda." He continued. "Yes, Edward C. White has given me the rudder of Handover Corp. I am the new CEO. My plan is to form a new board, and I'm looking for a fresh, innovative group of professional men and women who can help me move this company into the future. And yes, we will have a black-tie dinner in one month that will honor Mr. White, his board, and others who helped him establish Handover. All employees and their spouses are invited. It will be a grand event. Part of forward movement is to honor the past."

"One final thing," exclaimed Durham. "I want each one of you to brief your departments on what transpired today. Knowledge is power. Do not keep it to yourselves. Collaborative leadership requires sharing information. Is that clear?"

A collective "YES" resounded from the group. It reminded Brianna of the rafting trip.

After a few brief conversations, Brianna exited the conference room and hurried back to her office. She nearly skipped. *This is so exciting. I can't wait to tell the guys what happened this morning.*

The foursome had lunch together as Brianna briefed them on the morning's meeting.

"Awesome," responded Nate.

"I'm glad we will honor Mr. White and his board of directors," said George.

"It all sounds good," declared Brad. "But what happens when White is really gone? Time will tell."

Thirty days later, the gala event transpired. A regal dinner was served in the ballroom of a snazzy downtown hotel—resplendent with chandeliers, champagne, and waiters galore. Edward C. White looked stately in his black tuxedo sitting at the head table with many of his former colleagues. As soon as dessert was served, White stood up and gave his final address to the Handover employees. His tanned but worn face revealed a mixture of sadness and satisfaction.

At just the right time, he called Peter Durham to the podium, reiterated his credentials, and gushed about the changes he was already making at Handover. "I cannot commend him highly enough," asserted White. And then, as a final symbolic gesture, Edward C. White handed Peter Durham the keys to his executive office. "I trust you, Peter; take us forward. You're the captain of the ship now."

A thunderous roar of applause filled the room. White extended his hand to Durham, and Peter gave Edward a warm embrace. The transfer was complete. The founder and CEO of Handover Corp. had stepped down.

What does it mean to let go of executive leadership? Edward C. White made the monumental decision to step aside, but only time will tell how he will react when Handover hits turbulent waters. Will Peter Durham really have the freedom to lead *his* way? What kind of relationship should they have? Should Edward White still give input? If so, how often and in what ways? The transition from one executive leader to another is challenging, similar to the raw power and unpredictability of white water. When that process involves a founder, it can be like navigating the force and intensity of the "Bus Stop." Extremely careful planning is required.

Leadership transition is concerned with succession—the question of who should succeed an existing leader. Which person (or persons) is best for the longevity and future viability of an organization? This question is vital to the overall health and endurance of any group, of course. But when the process involves a founding leader, the issues can be even more profound. In their book *Family Business Succession*, authors Aronoff, McClure, and Ward refer to the process as "the final test of greatness."[1]

Managing the leadership transition process is certainly complex, having multiple layers of issues—many of which are hidden under the surface, like boulders in a river. Organizational culture, personalities, and generational issues, along with hopes and dreams, are involved. CEOs, especially those who are founders, have to deal with relinquishing control and with what might have been. They must face both accomplishments and disappointments as well as their own mortality. The emotional process can be incredibly painful.[2]

This is also a strategic time to reassess an organization, considering vision, global trends, areas of challenge, and what kind of leadership (values, style, attributes) is needed for future growth and development. Because of this complexity and the time required to assess appropriately, many researchers who focus on organizational development emphasize the need for advance planning. A solid leadership transition proposal is paramount, including the systematic and strategic transfer of skills and knowledge to others.[3]

Unfortunately, research also highlights the lack of appropriate planning for leadership succession.[4] In fact, "Hundreds of thousands of businesses across the nations are approaching the retirement or death of their founders or chief executives with no plans for succession or inadequate plans that will fail to produce the desired results."[5]

Many of these are family businesses. Why? Aronoff, McClure, and Ward declare, "Few challenges demand more of a business owner than passing on the family business to the next generation. Family members' lifelong hopes, dreams, ambitions, relationships, even personal struggles with mortality—all figure into managing succession."[6] These types of issues can also be found in the nonprofit sector, where many workers are volunteers who do not fit within the typical business control structure.[7]

A particular challenge facing many organizations is the strong culture left behind by the founder. According to Edgar Schein, such an organizational culture must be understood so that an intelligent transition occurs, allowing for the changeover to succeeding generations to occur in a way in which "the organization remains adaptive to its changing external environment without destroying the cultural elements that have made it unique."[8]

Founders may find it troubling that the next generation is creating a new structure, one that is completely different from the system with which they were comfortable. Organizational founders tend to operate "leader-central." Their power is dominant; everybody comes to them for direction. Then suddenly the new executive leader is making decisions via consensus or creating an outside board of directors. Founders can feel threatened. Handing over the rudder of leadership is such a paradigm shift for them. These folks can be tempted to stay involved too long or to step back in, taking the helm once again when the organization hits rough waters. Founders must keep in mind that their final goal is to create an organization that can sustain itself even when they are no longer around.[9]

What are some of the key challenges in such an executive leadership transition? The first one is determining whether the transition is real or theoretical. As one Boomer executive described it during my research: "Oftentimes my experience has been that transition is theoretical, not real—where we live every day. So even people who have said 'Yes, I have transitioned out of leadership,' when you look closely—yeah, someone else has been named as leader, but they are still doing it from behind the scenes. And in my opinion, that is not a transition of leadership."[10]

Another challenge, especially for organizations that still have their founding leadership, can be the reality of "oral tradition." In other words, the organization is lacking in written documentation—functioning almost like a paperless society. When the time comes for the founder to step down, organizational structure, job descriptions, and policies have to be clarified and documented. If not, there can be much ambiguity and confusion.

Appropriate transition requires mentoring, which is especially desired by the Gen Xers and Millennials. One Gen X leader remarked, "We need people to cover us and walk with us through the process. . . . I realize that I want to be mentored, to go to someone who is not critical or judgmental of me, but will mentor me, give wise discernment, and give me the bigger picture."[11] Another Gen Xer added, "I definitely don't think leadership should be passed on without a transition time, a time of teaching."[12]

An executive from the Silent cohort focused on the necessity of values: "The key to appropriate transition is the passing on of beliefs and values. . . . Through every generation we want to see the beliefs and values held to but new expressions of programs to come forward."[13] A Gen Xer agreed: "I'm talking about the passing along of real responsibility and decision making but in conjunction with the values. I think my generation is dangerous if you just give them a platform without the principles."[14]

The final challenge in any leadership transition, especially when founders step down, is how to cope with the inevitable tension that will arise. One Boomer leader summarized it insightfully: "We will rise and fall on our capacity to deal with tension. . . . That is the issue for us; how are we going to deal with tension? How do we ask the questions? How do we talk about these questions? How do we come to a consensus? We are going to miss [the founders]; there is nobody like them. The question is: Are we going to work together?"[15]

The next eighteen months brought many changes to Handover Corp. Although it took a while, a new board of directors had been chosen. Durham had selected carefully, and it showed. He surrounded himself with bright men and women who were also known for their moral integrity. Board meetings were dynamic, engaging, and quite productive. The group had tremendous synergy, thanks to a solid mix of risk-takers, implicational thinkers, and hands-on application folks. Some changes had been made with department leaders as they met faithfully with Durham each Monday morning. Peter had even sent more departmental groups white-water rafting to support team building.

Peter Durham was tackling the challenges of globalization and was trying hard not to outsource the work. George and Brad still had their jobs. The greatest challenge to navigate had been the stock price. Although Handover was not a publicly traded company, it did offer stock; and its price had been in decline for a number of months.

Durham was not worried.

However, someone else was also watching the downward trend.

PART THREE

Navigating the Rapids

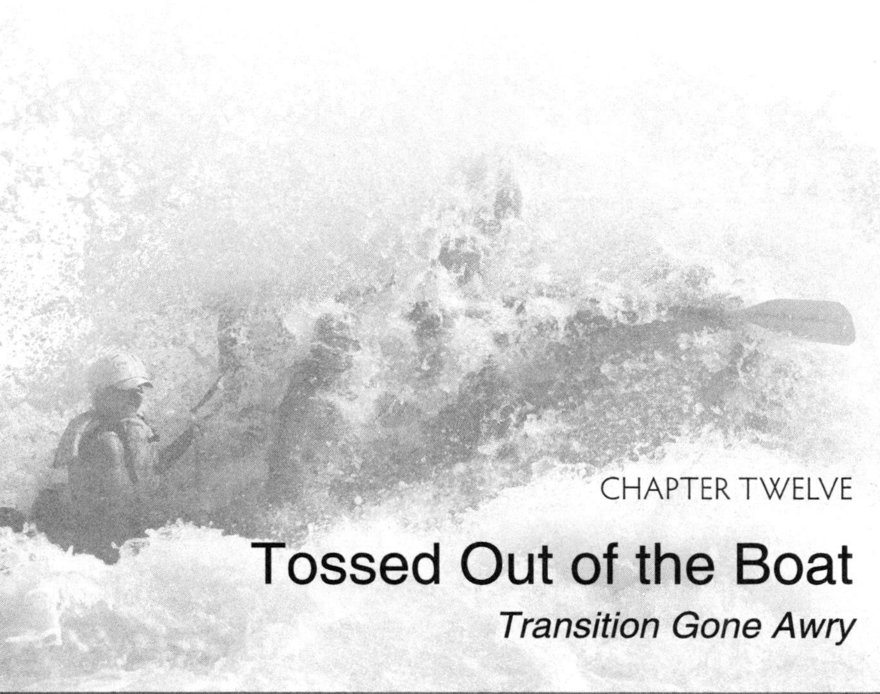

CHAPTER TWELVE

Tossed Out of the Boat

Transition Gone Awry

Edward C. White grimaced as he browsed Handover's current financials. Peter Durham sent him quarterly updates. The stock price continued to decline. He was not happy. No, he was in distress. What if the company went into an economic tailspin? They could lose everything. His parents had lived through the Great Depression. Innovation was great, but one had to remain true to the original values of the company. Financial prudence was paramount. The all-too-familiar thoughts began their daily jog through his mind. *What is Peter thinking? I trusted him, but perhaps I chose the wrong successor. His innovations are taking the company down a different path, and it is not working. Handover is adrift. I retired too early. What should I do?*

The leadership transition had occurred just eighteen months earlier, but these thoughts plagued White day and night. Handover was his baby. Conceived in his mind, he had nurtured it, given his life to it, and sacrificed for it. He had watched it rise from its humble beginnings in a garage to a respected mid-sized company in which people had invested—and continued to do so. Handover was not yet publicly traded, but Edward White's dream had always been the New York Stock Exchange.

By golly, he was not going to watch Handover disintegrate in front of his eyes. A radical intervention was needed, so that's what he would so. *Good thing I retained fifty-one percent of the company stock.* White reached for the phone.

In a bustling upscale gym on the other side of town, Peter Durham was jogging on a treadmill, watching the live Dow Jones ticker tape on MSNBC. He could hardly wait for Handover to be a publicly traded company. *Just another year or two.*

The treadmill began to slow automatically, bringing him back to his current reality. Handover's stock price was down again. He had grown accustomed to it. Peter had been involved in stocks for twenty years. There were so many variables. As Thomas Friedman illustrated in his book *The World Is Flat*, globalization has "flattened" the world and made the economic markets much more volatile. The modifications Durham was making at Handover would take some time to gel. Things would get better. His head was bursting at the cranial seams with new ideas, and the people on his board were creative and innovative.

They had wonderful synergy together.

The only thing that really bugged Durham was the lack of communication from Edward C. White. They had agreed to stay in touch. He sent White the quarterly financial statements. *What is he thinking? Is he pleased with my leadership of Handover? I still want his counsel, but he seems distant. I guess no news is good news.*

He wiped his face and headed to the sauna. It was 8:00 A.M., and he wanted to be at the office by 9:00. This job energized him.

By 10:00 A.M. Edward C. White had organized a conference call with some of the folks with whom he had pioneered the company. He had fond memories of working together in his garage—mapping out the company vision and watching it grow. As their voices came on the line, he breathed a sigh of relief. *Yes, I can trust these people.*

After a few pleasantries, Edward White got right to the point. Handover was in trouble. He shared with them the current stock price and the downward trend of the past months. They all agreed that this was disconcerting. Although all of them were either retired or serving as consultants for various companies and projects, Edward C. White laid out an SOS plea: return to Handover and work with him to put the company back on track. He asked them to get back to him within a week.

Back at the office, Peter Durham was meeting with his board of directors. As he scanned the faces around the conference table, he was once again amazed at the talented people working with him. These men and women in their thirties and forties were vibrant and self-motivated. Although the stock price was down, this group was not dismayed at all; but rather they were confident and more motivated than ever to steer the company in new directions, building on the solid foundations laid by Edward C. White. Their collective goal was to see Handover publicly traded on the New York Stock Exchange.

Durham had initiated the weekly meetings with department leaders, but recently selected board members had joined them. He used collaboration to connect the executives, middle managers, and employees. Decision making had been greatly enhanced. No one was in the dark. Brianna, representing IT, was still part of that initiative. It had taken a while to adjust to the retirement of the founder, but most of the Handover employees were encouraged by the changes. It reminded Brianna of the tranquil waters between rapids. Little did she and the others know how soon the next rapid would appear.

One week later, Edward C. White had the answers he wanted. Some of his old crew would return to help him right the company, reverting to the tested ways of the past. He wasted no time. One phone call would change everything. He dialed the number to Peter Durham's office. Peter's administrative assistant put him through immediately.

"Mr. White, how are you? Haven't heard from you in a while," said Peter. He was oblivious.

"Hello, Peter," replied Edward C. White. "How are things going?" *Maybe he will admit that things are looking bleak and this will be easier.*

"Things are going great!" responded Peter. "I have a fantastic board of directors who are willing to engage with my department leaders. We have a wonderful dynamic going. The transition has gone well, and I am very optimistic. Now if I can just get the stock price to cooperate," he said with a chuckle. *I'm glad he finally called.*

"Glad you mentioned that, Peter, because I am concerned about the financial viability of the company. The stock price has been falling consistently. We may start losing investors." White's voice inflection was somber.

"I'm not worried," replied Peter, a bit taken back by the tone of Mr. White's voice. "The financial statements don't give the whole picture. You know how volatile the business markets can be. Do you have any suggestions?" *I really do want his feedback.*

Edward C. White took a deep breath. *I wish there was another way. But there isn't. I have to do this.* "Peter, I am sorry to have to do this, but for the sake of the company I must ask you to resign immediately. Your board of directors will also need to step down. The current financial situation is too tenuous, and as the founder I have to intervene."

Peter Durham sat frozen in his chair, the last few sentences still trying to register in his brain. *He can't be serious. Such an abrupt change will create chaos. Who will lead things? Surely he will listen to reason.*

Durham struggled to remain calm, but anger crept up his back and neck. "Mr. White, with all due respect, why haven't you called me earlier to express your concerns? You haven't called in months. And now you want to just fire me? I beg you to reconsider." He could hear the edge in his own voice.

"Peter, I'm sorry; but I have to do this. Your innovations have placed Handover at risk, and that is unacceptable to me and to the others who pioneered this company."

"Mr. White, give me three months," implored Durham. "The board and I will meet with you and the other founders. We can get through this. Why don't we meet for lunch and talk this over in person?"

Edward White didn't hesitate. He was resolute. "No, Peter. I'm so sorry, but I've made up my mind. I will issue a communiqué to the employees. You have one week to clear out your office. We will buy out the remainder of your contract, and I'm sure you'll find the right company to lead." *This unpleasant task is almost over. I am back at the helm, and I will do whatever it takes to get Handover productive and vibrant once again.*

Edward C. White was finished. There was nothing more to say.

Peter Durham was stunned and in shock. His emotions were all over the map. All he could muster on the phone was a simple "All right. I'll take care of it." He hung up the phone and stared into space for almost an hour. *How can this be happening to me? I had so many great offers eighteen months ago. And I turned them down for this?*

The following week was like a B-grade movie: action taking place but with no sense of continuity. Peter Durham cleaned out his desk, tossed his visions for the company in the trash, notified his board, and talked with only a few employees. He felt humiliated. The company communiqué appeared first thing Monday morning in the inbox of every employee.

Attention, all employees of Handover Corp. You may be aware that in the last months the stock price of Handover has fallen consistently. This is unacceptable. In consultation with others who helped found this great company, I have decided to step back in as CEO. Peter Durham and his board of directors have been asked to resign effective immediately.

I know that you have already been in transition, but for the sake of the company I am asking for your cooperation in this difficult time. I am establishing a new board of directors made up of people who helped me in the beginning. We will be meeting with department heads in the coming weeks to reorganize and place things back on track. Thank you for your cooperation.

Edward C. White, Founder and CEO

Nate, Brad, Brianna, and George read the e-mail that morning and met for coffee at their normal Monday "preview of the week" meeting they had been having since Peter Durham took over as CEO. They looked as stunned and shaken as they had after "Disaster Falls." How could they ever forget the white-water wave that slapped Brianna overboard in an instant?

"Dude, what happened?" remarked Nate, the first one of the four to speak. "I thought things were going pretty well. The innovations were awesome."

"It's all about the bottom line," said Brad. "The company stock price has been falling, and the old man freaked. Simple as that."

"This makes me really nervous," Brianna remarked, as she

joined the dialogue. "First we go through the shock of the founder stepping down, the near-fiasco with Daniel Batten, and then Peter Durham. It has taken all of the past eighteen months to get reorganized and used to the changes. Now this. We've become more collaborative and inclusive in our decision-making process. The board of directors now includes women. Why are we going backward?"

George attempted to bring some comfort. "Hey, don't forget how Mr. White dealt with Daniel Batten. I don't understand this, but I trust him. He knows what he's doing, and he deserves our loyalty and support."

"Trust is earned," quipped Brianna.

"Ditto," said Brad. "I've never trusted authority figures, anyway."

"Whatever," chimed Nate. "Life is dynamic; nothing stays the same. Let's see what happens."

Transitions. Although they can be planned for and directives can be given, sometimes they go awry. The process can hit some very rough waters and simply not go as intended. Organizational flow charts mapping out a changeover do not predict the human fallout from transitions, especially when the transition has major implications. What can possibly go wrong during a transition?

Change Is Not Transition

One of the greatest mistakes made in organizational shifts is assuming that change is the same as transition. It is not. A quiet mountain stream is not the same as an undulating rapid. The only thing they have in common is water. Change and transition are similar, but change is situational.

- A new CEO comes on board.
- A pastor is voted out.
- A new leader is assigned to a work group.
- The organizational vision is modified.
- A founder steps down.
- Work is outsourced, and people are laid off.

All of these changes are situational. In other words, they are factual. Something changed. But transition represents the kind of change that results in powerful emotions. Edward White feels insecure. Peter Durham is confused and angry. Daniel Batten's vision of becoming the next CEO was dashed when an outsider was brought in to take the helm. Brad is wary of authority. Brianna is nervous. Nate is tentative. With the organization restructuring, George may have to retire; so he is apprehensive. Each of these individuals is experiencing valid feelings. They will each face difficult heart choices as they navigate the transition. Will they become bitter and cynical? Are they able to forgive? Will they find the inner strength to move on?

There is a psychological process that people go through to process transition, and it can be as unpredictable as a raging river. The more radical the shift, the more random and volatile the reactions can be. In his book *Getting Them Through the Wilderness: A Leader's Guide to Transition*, William Bridges talks about three phases people experience when they are dealing with transition: ending, the neutral zone, and new beginnings.[1] Diane Decker and James Belohav refer to these stages as disengaging, realigning, and initiating.[2] Regardless of terminology, both of these sources acknowledge that transition does not take place without recognizing the human factor.

In other words, there is a progression from accepting the fact that something has ended to stepping into fresh opportunities. People must come to terms with leaving the past behind, accepting an uncomfortable transitory state of confusion and uncertainty, and embracing new realities. It is not easy, and it takes time.

Researchers assert that organizational transition leads to a plethora of responses in people ranging from uncertainty, fear, depression, and confusion to excitement and enthusiasm. When transition involves the exit of a leader, studies find that people may feel hope, fear of abandonment, and/or anxieties about the impact of change on their careers.[3] In the midst of the turbulence of an organizational shift, some people may begin to disengage internally from the company. Their commitment level declines.

If human emotions are not taken into consideration and change is simply executed, transition can be devastating. An organization can literally come to a standstill in the process, hitting the rocks of disorientation. Sharp drops in productivity may occur; along with plummeting morale—or even the death of a vision. In some situations great damage can occur to people, leaving them scarred and hesitant to continue the journey with their organization or even in the same vocation.

Absence of Dialogue and Grief

Another common mistake in the transition process is avoiding dialogue. Change is announced and implemented but little room is given for discussion—that is, processing emotions, differences of opinion, and personal pain. Instead, the focus is on the new vision, a change of direction, and forward movement; and the expectation is that people will get in the boat and keep paddling.

Although people may be going through the motions of transition, powerful emotions can be swirling underneath the surface. When there is no dialogue or space to process at the affective level, these emotions are prolonged.

By now you may wonder why an organization would avoid such a process. The answer is that it is painful and messy and requires time. Oftentimes a group finds it easier to avoid this process and move on. Although their raft carries wounded or dead bodies on board, they just don't talk about them.

If a loss occurs in the midst of transition, people naturally go through a grieving process. Loss of title, position, or money obviously results in grief. However, there are other profound losses that are like rock formations hidden beneath the surface—the kind that can trap rafters and even kill them.

- Loss of identity
- Loss of trust and respect for leadership
- Loss of colleagues

- Loss from no longer having a voice or influence
- Loss of hope, purpose, and vision

Similar to the disorientation of a thunderous white-water rapid, a person can feel literally lost in transition.

The grief progression often begins with shock and denial—"This cannot be happening"—and quickly moves to anger, sadness, resentment, fear, and panic.

"What is going to happen to me?"

"How am I going to support my family?"

"I can't believe they treated us this way."

"After all these years of service this is what we get?"

Depression can follow, accompanied by feelings of confusion, disillusionment, isolation, hopelessness, and despair.

"I don't understand."

"I used to believe in this company."

"I guess all organizations are the same; you can't trust anyone."

"I have no idea what to do."[4]

When the loss is particularly great, people can remain in this trough of darkness for a long time. When folks begin to surface again, they may be tentative, fearful, ambivalent, and easily offended. Once again, this process is normal and is in proportion to the harm done.

In Patrick Lencioni's book *The Five Dysfunctions of a Team*, absence of trust and fear of conflict are highlighted as the two factors that lead to the breakdown of a team. If people are no longer willing to trust and the group is incapable of "engaging in an unfiltered and passionate debate of ideas," things begin to disintegrate. Eventually people fail to commit anymore. They avoid accountability, and details fall through the cracks. Productivity declines. Relationships are strained, and the effectiveness of the team is greatly diminished.[5] Consider the effectiveness of an organization when these types of losses begin to pile up. In the world of white-water rafting, this spells disaster. And so it is in any organization.

Lack of Implicational Thinking

A third mistake in organizational transition is a lack of implicational thinking. In rafting, there is no turning back once you put the boat in the water and the white water begins. If the guide has no plan for navigation and simply takes things as they come, the consequences can be severe. In the tumultuous rapids of transition, many times there is little or virtually no planning for the aftermath of the original change. People, positions, vision statements, and history are tossed to and fro, with organizations losing time in continual rebuilding, reinventing, and redoing. There can even be a loss of continuity and heritage, with no connection from one leader to another.

This scenario is like the "Bus Stop," the rapid that literally picks up a raft and tosses it around and around. Forward movement is virtually impossible until the raft manages to pop loose. Some never do. The only way to navigate the "Bus Stop" effectively is to plan for it in advance, carefully advising the rafters to paddle to the far edge of the rapid and avoid the chaos of the middle.

Lack of Appropriate Closure

One of the most vital elements in a successful transition is closure. People need an opportunity to disengage, relinquish roles, and be recognized for what they have done. Farewells and expressions of thanks are imperative. Can you imagine a group not celebrating at the end of a triumphant rafting trip? They may never see the rafting guide again, but they will thank him or her profusely. And vice versa. It takes an entire team effort to traverse the rapids.

In an organization's rush to move on, however, appropriate closure often doesn't happens. Positions change, flow charts adjust, people come and go, but closure is missing. This can plunge people into utter chaos emotionally. Almost overnight, responsible and reputable folks are without title or status—cast into the chaos of transition—and their contribution is not acknowledged. The results can be deep disillusionment, loss of self-esteem, grief, isolation, and despair. Although many of these feelings accompany any transition, some of the edge can be tempered by simply planning for closure. It is a matter of honor.

Loss of Truth-tellers

Finally, the supreme damage in any organizational transition comes from losing truth-tellers, those who dare to speak up even when others disagree. The rafting guide is counting on each participant to say what he or she sees. Many dangers are hidden, and the guide cannot see them all. Unfortunately, loyalty sometimes takes precedence over truth in the midst of transition; and the truth-tellers are silenced. The raft crashes head-on into the boulder in the mist of the raging waters, and no one says anything. Inconceivable.

In his article "Honoring the Truth-teller," Roger Sapp talks about loyalty-based organizations and the various types of people in them. In such an organization, whether it is a church, business, or nonprofit, the dominant value is loyalty to authority—no matter what transpires or how unjustly people are treated. Some people allow themselves to be abused. They may complain behind closed doors, but they do nothing productive to deal with the problem. Others offer feedback and try to confront situations and negotiate. If such efforts are ignored, rebuffed, or judged harshly, these folks may withdraw and refuse to cooperate. In many cases, however, they are labeled as rebels and blamed for withdrawing. Organizational troubles are defended, and truth is distorted by placing a politically correct spin on it. Every time loyalty prevails over truthfulness, faithful people are unintentionally taught to hide the truth. The message to truthful people is that they are not really welcome. An organizational blindness can develop.[6]

Groups are especially vulnerable in times of transition. If honest feedback is not allowed, the truth-tellers will begin to leave the organization and move on—which is tragic, because these types of people can help an organization deal with its problems and grow. The irony is that both loyalty and truth are vital within an organization. Loyalty unites people and fosters teamwork. The truth sets us free from deception. Loyalty and truth combined can result in true unity with integrity.

Organizational transition cannot afford to be one-dimensional. Much more than simply adjusting an organizational diagram or considering outcomes, transitions deal with human beings who have unique personalities, personal histories, and cultural backgrounds as well as generational similarities. Giving people appropriate time to process, allowing for dialogue, providing closure, and having a plan to guide the transition can make a huge difference. Otherwise, the experience is likely to be referred to as "Disaster Falls."

Gathering later for lunch in the company cafeteria, the foursome sat in silence, as did many others. Stillness hung over the eatery like a heavy cloud on a hot, humid summer day. What was there to say? It was a done deal, and this time there was no one to appeal to. They would simply have to ride it out. Over the next weeks and months they would feel as if they were rafting down the Black River all over again—but without a guide. Emotions would rage, relationships would be strained, and trust and respect would be tested like never before.

They waited for the next communiqué from Edward C. White.

CHAPTER THIRTEEN

Who Has the Rudder?

Transition Can Be Chaotic

The next e-mail broadcast from White's office came later that day. Short and to the point, it did not reveal much.

> Attention, all employees—and especially department leaders. Please be patient as we reorganize. As soon as we have a plan in place we will call a staff meeting. Until then, it is vital that each one of you continue with your normal responsibilities. If you have any questions, please contact my office. Thank you for your service to Handover Corp.
>
> Edward C. White, Founder and CEO

"Who's the corporate 'we'?" asked Brad, his voice laced with sarcasm. "It doesn't look like the department heads are involved in real leadership anymore."

"Maybe it's only for a season," replied Brianna. Her tone did not reflect a lot of hope.

"C'mon, you all. Perk up," said George. "We're in good hands. These are the guys who started Handover."

"I don't know. Seems awful secretive to me," exclaimed Nate. "What's to hide?"

The remainder of the week seemed agonizingly slow. People wandered around like they were in a fog—taking care of details but not really all there. They were going through the motions but devoid of enthusiasm. It was weird.

Brianna saw a number of her departmental colleagues at lunch or in the hallway. *I miss the collegiality we had in those planning meetings with Peter Durham. I feel lost.* When others opened up, similar thoughts and emotions came spilling out.

Finally, another e-mail arrived, announcing an employees' meeting for Monday morning at 9:00 A.M. The new organizational plan would be unveiled. No one had a clue.

As they filed into the large meeting area Monday morning, Brianna couldn't help but notice the stark difference in the setting. It felt stiff and formal. Edward C. White and his colleagues were seated up front at a large table, facing the rest of the group. They all had gray hair. The employees sat in rows like obedient schoolchildren in a classroom, waiting for the teacher to present the lesson. No whiteboard or small groups today. *Give it a chance, girl.*

Edward White began with the history of the company, complete with PowerPoint and a timeline. The longer he talked, the more excited he became. Peter Durham's name was not even mentioned. Then he introduced each of the new board members. They were obviously close friends of Mr. White, those whom he trusted.

Brianna fumed inwardly. *I respect him so much. He built this company, bringing vision to reality. He was kind to me when I went to him about Daniel Batten. But I'm so angry with him right now. God help me.*

Finally, he projected the new organizational flow chart onto the screen. Each board member had executive oversight of a particular department and was directly accountable to the CEO. The department heads, those who carried out the daily responsibilities, were missing on the chart. Chatter flowed through the group like a river rapid.

At that point, Edward White grabbed the microphone. "Calm down, everyone. Let me explain." A collective hush filled the room.

"You have to understand something," he began. "My role as CEO is only temporary. Maybe two to three years, five at the most. We must make the shift to younger leadership for future viability but not without the principles and ethics of Handover Corp. The board and I are responsible to cultivate future leadership. For that reason we will be appointing new department leaders in the next few weeks. Some of you will remain in that position; others will be new. Work with us. We'll keep you informed."

The meeting came to an end. No dialogue. It was back to command and control.

In the weeks that followed, numerous "mini-transitions" occurred within departments. A number of young Gen Xers filled middle management roles. Brianna kept her position as head of IT, but things were definitely different. Although she was "in the know" about some things, in other ways she was shut out. The real power rested at the top, and it was frustrating to carry responsibility with no real authority. No one knew how long this would continue.

At the end of one particularly exasperating day when Brianna was caught between the rocks of responsibility and the rapids of corporate confusion, she sat at her desk and cried in utter frustration. The three guys couldn't help but hear her. They eased into her office.

"What's wrong?" George queried in his fatherly voice.

"I can't take it anymore," she replied, fighting back tears. "I'm stressed out and angry, and it is taking a toll on my family."

"You should go down to the arcade and play that whack-a-mole game," Nate suggested, trying to inject some humor. "When I'm really stressed, I give the moles specific names and just clobber them."

Brianna laughed out loud.

"Sounds good to me," exclaimed Brad, with a grin.

The foursome looked at each other and smiled. "My gosh!" declared Brianna. "We've sure been through a lot. And it all started at Black River. At least we've got each other."

The three guys nodded in unison.

"Low in the boat," Brad quipped with a commanding voice.

"LOW IN THE BOAT!" shouted the others.

"Somehow, we'll navigate through this rapid," declared Nate.

The foursome smiled broadly. *Where was Daniella when you needed her?*

It would be easy to create a fairy-tale ending to this story. But in reality the future of this fictional company and its employees is yet to be determined. It will hinge on leadership—and more specifically on leadership transition.

Although there are many examples of poor transitions in various organizations, research indicates that a good transition is possible. Major corporations, start-up companies, nonprofit agencies, and other groups have modeled it. What are the dynamics of a good leadership transition, particularly from one generation to another? How will you implement these insights and principles in your organization?

Take your place in the raft. Read on. The journey isn't over yet.

CHAPTER FOURTEEN

Staying in the Raft

Good Transitions Are Possible, but They Must Be Deliberate

Could you identify with George, Brad, Brianna, or Nate? Maybe the woes of Peter Durham struck a nerve in you. Or perhaps you related to Edward White. Each one experienced the transition at Handover in a unique way. Maybe you could not relate at all. Whatever the case, one thing is certain: If you have not yet experienced a transition in leadership in your company, family business, church, volunteer association, or nonprofit group, one is coming your way. And it could be just as wild as a white-water rapid!

Leadership transition is part of life. The question of who

should succeed an existing leader, especially the founder, is vital to the longevity, overall health, and future viability of any organization. Although this would seem to be common sense, research suggests that there is a critical lack of appropriate planning for leadership succession.[1]

Even more riveting, however, are the current global trends that demand new generations of innovative and quality leadership. Let's consider a few of them.

Some Pressing Global Trends

In his book *Managing in the Next Society*, world-renowned expert Peter Drucker delineated several factors that are changing society and will continue to make an impact for decades. Consider how the following information might affect your organization as it considers the future.

A Shrinking Young Population

One of the most stunning factors is the shrinking young population globally. In every developed country, the birthrate is now well below the replacement rate of 2.2 live births per woman of reproductive age. China and Brazil have similar trends. To appreciate the implications of this trend, consider the nation of Germany. By 2030 almost half of the adult population in that nation will be over the age of sixty-five.[2]

The impact of this demographic shift will be staggering. New employment patterns will have to be created that keep the growing number of older people in the workplace. To add to the mix, many of these older workers will not be traditional 9 to 5 employees but rather key contributors as consultants, temporaries, part-timers, and people on special assignments. Drucker believed that by about 2025 as many as half of the people who work for a business will not be employed by it, at least not full-time.[3] *How does this information weigh in as you clarify the vision for your organization?*

The Internet and Rise of E-Commerce

Other dynamics are the Internet and e-commerce, which has become a major worldwide distribution channel for goods, services, and jobs. Thomas Friedman's book, *The World Is Flat,* highlights this change, along with other innovations such as supply chaining, outsourcing, and the global shift to capitalism.[4] Drucker commented on this as well, pointing out that manufacturing is declining as the top producer of wealth and new jobs. It is being replaced by information technology. Combine e-commerce with the move toward new technologies and you have what Drucker referred to as the "next society."[5] *In what ways is your organization capitalizing on information technology and the Internet?*

A Brave New World

Another facet of the "next society" is that it has many new players. Friedman writes that around the year 2000 "a whole new group of people, several billion, in fact, walked out onto the playing field from China, India, and the former Soviet

Union."[6] The next society will require changes in the function and structure of the corporation and top management. *What will that kind of leadership look like?*

Executive leadership will face new demands. They have to accept global competition and form the necessary partnerships to compete. Partnerships present new challenges, however. True partners cannot be controlled but rather are collaborated with based on values, objectives, and expectations. In other words, the CEO of tomorrow will have to be able to understand when to partner, when to command, and, most importantly, how to negotiate.[7] *Are these skills evident in your leaders? If not, what plan do you have to develop them?*

In light of these trends, the demand for quality leadership transitions becomes palpable. What dynamics are most critical? Current literature and research indicate that solid transitions are possible, but they must be deliberate. Four key factors for success emerge:

- Clarify the vision of the organization.
- Establish a leadership succession plan.
- Consider people in the process.
- Factor in the generational differences in your working group.

Let's consider each of these factors in the context of your organization. Common issues exist, but the application will be unique. As each category is taken into account, specific questions are posed to help you process the information and work toward solutions, or at least ideas, to help with your particular situation.

Clarifying the Vision

Leadership transition brings an excellent opportunity to reexamine an organization, regardless of its nature. The group may be a business, church, educational or health care institution, humanitarian organization, nonprofit group, or a myriad of others. Whatever the type of organization, however, a sense of defining vision gives its reason for existence. You can find it in the mission statement. As vision is clarified, key questions are similar:

- What was your original organizational vision? Has it changed?
- How does the vision correspond to current global trends?
- What is the current state of your organization? Is it thriving?
- What are the areas of greatest tension or challenge?
- Has your group experienced a recent merger or other type of reorganization? If so, how does it affect your organizational vision?
- What is your organization's overall strategy for the future? Is it relevant?

- Does a new technology need to be introduced?
- What types of strategic partnerships might be helpful? Are you open to this?
- What kind of leadership (values, style, attributes) is needed for future growth and development?

A group might have a vision that was appropriate fifty years ago but does not resonate with these current global realities. The entire organization may need to be reexamined for relevance. In many instances, such an honest look at a group may lead to a "midlife crisis," but this appraisal is vital to the ongoing viability of any organization. Vision must be clarified. A strategic part of that process is to ask the hard questions. Times of leadership transition can bring many issues into focus if people are willing to take a candid and sincere overview of the organization: its history, context, values, and future in the current world situation.

Working through the vision and values of an organization is complex and has implications for every facet of the group, including people, leadership, products, services, and outcomes. If an organization wants to keep moving down the river successfully, however, the process of clarifying the vision is vital.

Succession Planning

Once the vision is clarified, a definite plan for leadership succession is key. In her book *Hesselbein on Leadership*, Frances Hesselbein, the former CEO of the Drucker Foundation for Nonprofit Management, makes a simple yet profound statement:

"Few events in the life of an organization are as critical, as visible, or as stressful as when the leader leaves the organization. Effective leaders plan an exit that is as positive and graceful as their entrance was."[8]

Numerous business experts agree that leaders should plan, communicate, and manage the period of leadership transition.[9] In 2004 a comprehensive review was conducted of recent research on succession planning. The results estimated that only 40–65 percent of organizations have a formal succession plan in place. The research also emphasized the importance of linking succession planning to the long-term strategic plans of the group.[10] Lack of appropriate planning in this area, however, is where many organizations "hit the rocks" while navigating the rapids of a transition.

Consider family businesses as an example. Research indicates that most family businesses do not survive into the second generation because of a failure to plan for leadership transition.[11] To appreciate fully the gravity of this point, an article in *Success* pointed out that the United States is in the midst of one of the greatest wealth transfers in its history. Although much of this wealth transfer will be in the form of family-owned businesses, it is estimated that only one out of three will be successfully transferred to the second generation.[12]

In another article, entitled "How to Plan for the Inevitable," an example is given of a small architectural firm that closed its doors within a short time after the unexpected death of the founder. No leadership transition plan existed for this firm. Why? The author of the article suggested that leadership transition planning is often viewed as demoralizing, the first step toward irrelevance.[13]

Major corporations are different. They tend to value intentional succession planning. Jack Welch, the former CEO of General Electric, began planning for his successor seven years before he planned to step aside at age sixty-five. During that period he identified his selection objectives, created a list of potential candidates, and had time to watch them closely. Welch wanted someone young enough to be the next CEO for at least a decade. The whole process was guided by careful thought and strategic planning.[14]

Once again, regardless of the type of working group, a succession plan is essential.

- Does your organization have a strategy for leadership succession? If not, what is your plan for creating one?
- If you have a leadership succession plan, in what ways have you factored in organizational culture? What might need to change?
- Which generations are currently represented in your group?
- In what ways have you factored in the generations in your leadership succession plan?
- What is your plan for systematically passing along the skills and knowledge necessary for the next generation of leaders in your organization?

Consider the People

Vision is clarified, and a succession plan is in place. Everything looks good on paper. Now what? The next step is to consider the people who will be affected by the change. The outworking of transition involves real human beings who have thoughts, feelings, futures, and a distinct generational imprint. Remember—leaders who have emotional intelligence recognize that there is a psychological process people go through to deal with transition.

Of course, much depends on the type of organization. In the corporate world people are salaried employees who are expected to go with the flow. Under Welch's leadership, performance was evaluated each year, and the worst performers (the bottom 10 percent) were cut.[15] It is not uncommon in some settings today for personnel to be informed of a layoff and expected to pack up their things immediately. But what does that communicate to those employees who are still with the company?

Drucker pointed out that nonprofits operate from a different motivation. Faith-based organizations often require their staff to raise their own financial support. In such situations, change and transition can be even more unsettling. Drucker stressed the need for trust, since nonprofit workers do not fit under the typical business control structure.[16]

Transitions involve people who have thoughts and feelings. They have invested time and effort into the group. Regardless of the type of organization, the human factor needs to be considered when planning and executing a transition.

- How emotionally intelligent is your organization? Your leadership?
- In what ways are you taking the human factor into consideration as you plan for a transition?

Generational Differences

The final step in planning a transition is accounting for the generational factor. Of course, that is the crux of this book. There is a better way to navigate leadership succession between the generations. Although the reality is that we've never been in this global situation before, all of the generations currently represented in the workforce are in this boat together. Not only does organizational vision need to be clarified and a succession plan developed, but they also must be done in context. Real people from distinct generations must be understood. The fictional story of Handover Corp. highlighted the challenge. George, Brad, Brianna, and Nate each had a unique perspective on leadership, depending on the generation in which they were raised. These generational differences are vital factors in any leadership transition.

Some companies have already made the leap. A good example is Genentech, voted the best company to work for in 2006. Consider the uniqueness of its organizational culture. Art Levinson, the CEO and a Baby Boomer, describes his company as "extremely nonhierarchical," a place where no one gets an assigned parking place or a fancy office. Collaboration is encouraged, success is celebrated, and people work hard. An on-site daycare center is available, along with other amenities that help people balance the demands of work and home. A job at Genentech is not easy to get. They screen out people who are focused on title, salary, and personal advancement. Genentech is looking for passionate people who are focused on research and results. Sounds like a place where Millennials can join, Gen Xers will thrive, and the Boomers and Silents can keep on going. Companies like Apple and Google are similar in nature.[17]

In their book *Generations at Work*, authors Ron Zemke, Claire Raines, and Bob Filipczak give additional positive examples, including Ben & Jerry's, T.G.I. Friday's, and Lucent Technologies. It is possible to navigate the generational differences and create a workplace in which each generation has a place of function and honor.[18]

- How multigenerational is your organization?
- In what ways are you helping people understand each other and work together across generational lines?
- Do changes need to be made to create a more cross-generational workplace? If so, what are they?
- How are you taking the generations into account as you plan for leadership transition?

As you consider these questions, keep in mind the points of tension between people from different generations—the places where they need help to understand one another and work together more effectively. Folks from the Silent Generation and the older Boomers tend to be task-oriented, are more familiar with a command-and-control type of leadership style, and anticipate automatic respect. Integrity is a high value for them.

Younger Boomers and Gen Xers tend to be more relational and desire a balance between task and relationship. They prefer a collaborative style of leadership, gathering input from others before making a final decision. For them, respect is earned rather than automatically given. Integrity is essential for these folks as well, but they are also looking for leaders who care and are willing to come alongside to mentor them.

Millennials are extremely relational and even more distanced from command and control. They tend to be ambitious and not afraid to question things. Commitment can be scary for them, so these young people prefer to fulfill shorter-term obligations. These younger members of the workforce prefer leaders who are dedicated but who also care about them personally.

During a leadership transition, a vast range of possible thoughts and feelings will affect each person, regardless of his or her generation. Older ones may fear being skipped over or forced out; younger ones will expect to be included in any decision-making process directly related to them. Each person will appreciate respect, plenty of communication, and caring concern. Tensions will arise, and relationships can become quite complicated. Just remember some of the interactions between George, Brad, Brianna, and Nate. However, when they moved beyond generational stereotypes and became acquainted as real people, they began to appreciate one another and really talk. Brad even apologized!

It takes effort to work through transition, especially with the multiple layers of personality, culture, organizational history, and generations. But it is possible. And understanding generational distinctions can make a significant difference during a time of leadership and organizational change.

As questions are considered in each of these four categories of clarifying vision, succession planning, considering people, and factoring in generational differences, it is always helpful to refer to some success stories. Let's take a look at some organizations that have successfully passed the oar of leadership from one generation to another. They have done it well; you can too.

CHAPTER FIFTEEN

Handing Over the Oar

Others Have Done It; You Can Do It Too

Some well-known companies have navigated major leadership transitions, handing over the rudder of leadership in the midst of a rapidly changing world and new business realities. Let's consider their examples as well as the challenge of their organizational cultures.

General Electric

The General Electric Company (GE) traces its roots back to Thomas Alva Edison, who established the Edison Electric Light Company in 1878. GE is the only company listed in the Dow Jones Industrial Index today that was also included in the original index in 1896. Innovation has always been the trademark of GE. However, the corporation had become highly bureaucratic by the time Jack Welch assumed leadership in 1981. Recognizing inflationary problems and the growing competition in Asia, Welch restructured GE.[1]

In his book *What the Best CEOs Know*, Jeffrey Krames writes, "Under [Welch's] direction, GE was transformed from an out-of-touch, $25 billion industrial manufacturer into an agile, $130 billion service juggernaut. . . . Recognizing the limits of the command and control hierarchies that ruled the day, Welch remade one of the world's largest bureaucracies into an organization that had learning and ideas at its heart."[2] GE became known for cost cutting, efficiency, continued improvement, and deal making. The company diversified into new areas, such as medical technologies, aircraft engines, and financial services.[3]

But GE's clarification of vision didn't stop there. The company went through another major leadership transition in 2001 when Jeffrey Immelt was appointed to replace Welch as CEO. Interestingly, he took office on September 7, just four days before the attack on the World Trade Center and the abrupt end of the bull market. As the new CEO of GE, he faced the daunting challenges of geopolitical instability, low growth, inflation, and the rise of China and India as competitors. These factors demanded many transitions.

Under Immelt's leadership the dominant characteristic is, once again, innovation. His leaders must submit three "imagination breakthrough" proposals each year that will take GE to a new geographic area or into a new line of business or customer base. The corporation has expanded its business portfolio to include media, security, bioscience, pure water, and renewable energy.

Coupled with risk taking and sophisticated marketing, Immelt has led a transformation of GE into a creative twenty-first-century global business force. The company motto is "Imagination at work, always with unyielding integrity." GE looks for employees who are curious, passionate, resourceful, accountable, committed, able to work in teams, and who are open and energizing. The very survival of GE has depended upon strategic transition, starting at the top.[4]

Wal-Mart

Wal-Mart started as a family business; Sam Walton opened his first store in 1962. He went up against the Goliaths of retail, such as Woolworth and Sears, entering the retail market with other newcomers like Kmart, Woolco, and Target. Walton's marketing plan was simple: low prices across the board with small margins for profit. He developed his own distribution system and traveled by pickup or plane to buy directly from suppliers. Hardly anyone took notice at first, but by 1979 Wal-Mart had 276 stores, 21,000 employees, and $1 billion in sales. By the late 1980s Wal-Mart was one of the most successful retailers in the United States.[5]

Sam Walton gave major attention to his succession plan. Unlike many family businesses that cash out when the founder dies or bring in a new CEO from outside the company, the

Walton family allowed the control to pass to a professional management team that Sam Walton himself had installed. He selected Rob Walton, his oldest son, to become the chairman of Wal-Mart, but David Glass became CEO.[6]

When David Glass took over as CEO in 1988, he built on Sam Walton's vision and values, but he added a highly efficient global supply chain—an innovation that made Wal-Mart a worldwide contender and one of the largest international corporations.[7] A significant difference between Walton and Glass is noteworthy. Walton, born in 1918, was a product of the Depression and a member of the World War II generation. He was concerned about debt and was not eager to embrace new technologies. Glass, however, was born in the midst of the Silent Generation and was more comfortable with increasing debt in order to build the company. He also capitalized on technology to fuel the logistics of a massive supply chain.

Organizational Culture and Succession

The strong culture left behind by the founder is a challenge facing many organizations. Consider how daunting it would be to follow in the footsteps of Jack Welch or Sam Walton. The new leader must be his or her own person, nonetheless, and be free to evaluate the organizational culture within the transition process. Each group has a unique culture, which can be positive at the beginning but become a liability in the future. The new leader has to navigate the nuances.

Looking back at Wal-Mart, it is clear that Sam Walton created a culture. Three basic beliefs supported that culture: respect for the individual, service to the customers, and striving for excellence. His goal was to raise the standard of living for his customers by offering rock-bottom prices. He introduced the Wal-Mart concept of "the rollback," an ongoing crusade to lower prices on household goods. Walton wanted everyone to be motivated and feel a part of the culture. The Wal-Mart cheer is legendary and can be seen throughout the world at every Wal-Mart store.[8]

Robert Slater, author of *The Wal-Mart Decade*, asserts, "The culture at Wal-Mart celebrates Sam Walton, but it was David Glass who had a global vision that allowed Wal-Mart to grow in ways that few expected. It was Glass who took Wal-Mart out of Middle America and made it a global brand, turning it into one of the largest corporations in the world."[9]

Regardless of how you may view Wal-Mart and some of its business practices, you cannot deny that the culture of the company has been proven to work throughout the world. The new leadership made changes that allowed for global growth and development, but the unique cultural elements of the organization remained. Wal-Mart is an important example of a successful leadership transition amid a healthy, ongoing company culture.

A different example would be IBM. In his book *Who Says Elephants Can't Dance?* Lou Gerstner talks about the historic turnaround of IBM, a company that nearly collapsed in the early 1990s. As the new CEO, Gerstner quickly discovered a stifling culture that prohibited growth. Bureaucracy was rampant, departments competed against each other, and some of the best and brightest up-and-coming managers were serving as administrative assistants. As an outsider, Gerstner had to learn the culture of IBM and then make strategic changes that allowed the company to thrive once again. In this situation, the company culture itself had become a blockade.[10]

An entirely dissimilar example is Habitat for Humanity, a nonprofit organization that builds affordable housing in partnership with people in need. Millard Fuller, who founded Habitat for Humanity in 1976, had issues of conflict with the board of directors when it came time for him to transition out of leadership. Although he was turning seventy, he wanted to serve longer. This can be a unique challenge in the culture of the nonprofit sector, in which mandatory retirement may not be a factor. Founders of such organizations can be hesitant to step aside and turn things over to the next generation.[11]

The church world is not exempt from this process and its challenges. The Catholic Church, whose organizational culture does not allow priests or nuns to marry, is facing a leadership crisis in dealing with a lack of priests and nuns in certain parts of the world. In the United States, the Catholic population doubled between 1950 and 2001, but the number of priests increased by only 6 percent. Many parishes in America do not have a full-time priest.[12] In 1965 there were 180,000 nuns, whereas in 2001 there were only 80,000. The average age of nuns at that time was sixty-nine.[13] Who will replace them?

The organizational cultures found in Protestant churches are rapidly changing. Questions about women's roles and leadership requirements continue to surface, megachurches are setting new trends, and the "emerging church" movement is challenging tradition.

The parachurch world is being challenged by changes in commitment levels, as younger generations prefer to commit to shorter-term projects rather than a long-term assignment. Founding leaders of key organizations like Campus Crusade for Christ, Operation Mobilization, and the Billy Graham Association have handed over their leadership to another generation. Other parachurch groups will undergo significant transition in the coming years, challenging organizational cultures and raising questions about future leadership.

To stay in the raft while navigating the rapids of generational leadership transition is certainly possible, but it requires careful maneuvering. Lots of rocks are in the way! Many of them are hidden just below the surface. Whether seen or unseen, rocks are dangerous. They can prevent you from arriving at your intended destination. But clarity of vision, combined with a plan for leadership succession that cares for people and celebrates the four unique generations, will take an organization to a safe and healthy conclusion.

Are you ready to finish this journey? Well, hang on to your paddle as we navigate the last rapid together and look at a case study of leadership succession. The nonprofit organization selected is as wild as white water, with waves of various cultures and generations. Yet it managed to survive and thrive as the founder and international director handed his leadership over to the next generation. I can imagine that many in the group screamed "We've never done it that way before" as they headed into the thunderous roar of organizational transition. But they realized they were "in the boat together," kept paddling, and lived to tell the tale. So can you.

CHAPTER SIXTEEN

Finishing the Course

Successful Changeover

Author's Note: There are more failures than successes when it comes to leadership succession. A few high-profile companies were highlighted in the previous chapters, but the following organization came to my attention as a good example of a leadership changeover that was well-planned and well-executed. Here is the story.

Operation Mobilization began with a simple prayer. An American housewife named Dorothea Clapp asked God to touch the world through the lives of young people. She prayed specifically for the students in her local high school. The decade was the 1950s, when the Silent Generation was coming of age and the Baby Boomers were being born.

One of those students was George Verwer, a teenager who later heard Billy Graham speak at a meeting and committed his life to God. While in college, Verwer and two friends who met regularly to pray became troubled by the spiritual needs of the people of Mexico. In 1957 they sold some of their possessions, purchased copies of the Gospel of John, and spent the summer in Mexico. They kept going back. When Verwer and his friends graduated in 1960, they traveled to Spain and did the same type of work.[1] A current was forming.

The three friends gradually realized that God was leading them to mobilize others to do what they had been doing. By 1963 they had two thousand others working with them in summer teams throughout Europe. Today Operation Mobilization (OM), with a staff of over four thousand, is active in more than one hundred countries.[2] In 2007 OM celebrated its fiftieth anniversary with an organizational vision that is as strong and precise as ever: to motivate and equip people to share God's love with people all over the world. A river of people committed to a common cause.

As a nonprofit, Operation Mobilization has unique challenges. Each staff member is a volunteer who must raise his or her own financial support. No one receives a salary. OM's international scope requires that teams and projects be scattered across many nations and regions of the world. How does one lead such an organization? Can you see the white water forming?

It takes a visionary, entrepreneurial type of leader to steer such a group. George Verwer was that man. Although he was the founder, Verwer never wanted an executive leadership role. He was the man at the helm of the boat, but his passion was simple. He wanted to see lives transformed by the power of God and that reality reflected in the world. Nonetheless, he realized early on that executive leadership was needed, so he accepted the role of international director. Verwer held that position for forty-six years.[3] The rest is history—until he decided to step aside and let someone else assume that role. The navigation process began!

As stated in chapter 14, research shows that a successful leadership transition requires clarity of organizational vision, a definitive leadership succession plan, concrete ways to consider people in the process, and a strategy to deal with the unique generations working within the organization. How did Operation Mobilization navigate each of those rapids?

Organizational Vision

Although the original vision of Operation Mobilization has not changed, it has been clarified over time. The most noteworthy adjustments have taken place within the past ten to twelve years. From its inception, the group was committed to world evangelization. Now, however, the entire movement has become much more involved in social action, which reflected a shift in thinking by Verwer himself, who said to me in an interview, "We never understood the kingdom [of God] and how these two [evangelism and social action] worked together."[4]

The focus is now on transformation—seeing God at work in people's lives—through proclamation as well as deed. The organization is involved in projects that serve children at risk, abused women, the extremely poor, HIV/AIDS patients, pregnant women and their unborn children, people with impure water, and the environment.

Another shift occurred in the area of finances. For the first thirty years of the organization, no one spoke about finances. Now, as Verwer states, "God has taught us the biblical reality of fundraising . . . the beauty of seeing millions of dollars provided for his kingdom work."[5]

To say that George Verwer left behind an organizational culture is an understatement. His trademark is a world-map athletic jacket that he wears as he speaks to large crowds. He speaks with gripping passion about a needy world. As Verwer announced his decision to step down, he needed a successor with similar values—someone that the whole organization would embrace. Not an easy rapid to navigate.

A Plan for Leadership Succession

Similar to the leadership successions at GE and Wal-Mart, Verwer announced his decision to step aside five years before he actually did so. He was sixty years old when he announced his decision. In our interview, Verwer stated, "I had read horror stories of those who hung on too long."[6] He wanted the whole organization to realize that leadership could not be contained at the top but needed to be broadened to include younger leaders in the leadership structure. Verwer decided that he would not pick his successor but rather would allow the movement itself to choose the new person. Such a decision was radical, especially from a founding leader, and was similar to navigating the "Bus Stop": everyone had to paddle hard to avoid the potential whirlpool of mistakes that could bring the organization to a standstill—dead in the water.

Names were submitted for consideration throughout Operation Mobilization, which generated discussion and interaction within the organization around the world.[7] Executive meetings were held. The man chosen to be the next international director was Peter Maiden, a colleague of Verwer's who was ten years younger, an early Boomer. Maiden joined OM in 1974 and had served as Verwer's associate international coordinator since 1985.[8]

Another stunning point is that Verwer completely stepped out of all leadership after he resigned. He did not serve on any board or have any direct executive authority. Verwer would not even accept an advisory role. As Maiden put it when I interviewed him, "George never tried to come back in and take over or micromanage. He has only gotten involved at my request—and with great reluctance."[9]

When he stepped aside as international director, Verwer invested himself full-time in special projects and teaching. What happens when OM does things he does not like? Verwer simply said, "I let others take care of it. That is not my responsibility anymore."[10]

When I asked Verwer to comment on the challenges of the leadership transition, he identified issues common to such situations. Some people felt that he should stay on longer. Not everyone was content with the successor. Others pushed for more decentralization, with less power at the top and more authority regionally based. A few people left the organization.

Asked what he would do differently if he could navigate the transition again, Verwer said, "I think I would have discussed my decision to step down a bit more widely. I should have processed my thinking with more people before going to the bigger group."[11] In fact, he recounted that the idea to step down came to him during an airplane flight. Peter Maiden happened to be on the same plane, and Verwer got up, went to Peter's seat, and said, "Peter, I think that in five years I need to step out of leadership."[12]

When I asked Maiden about his thoughts on that spontaneous announcement, he replied, "Quite surprised. It is big for a founder to stand down voluntarily."[13]

Verwer also mentioned the tension between loyalty and truth, an aspect we examined in an earlier chapter of this book. He acknowledged that at one point in the transition process his loyalty to certain leaders had blinded him to truth. Some pushed for more decentralization, but Verwer realized that the complexity of the organization demanded that it be field led but internationally coordinated. As he so succinctly put it, "It is not a free-for-all."[14]

Finally, I asked Verwer about the next leadership succession. Interestingly, he responded that he felt it would be a greater challenge the next time around. His successor, Peter Maiden, was very well-known in the organization and had a reputation for integrity and wisdom. It was not hard to get unity on his appointment. Verwer thinks it may be difficult the next time, however, to achieve that kind of consensus in an organization that is so widespread.[15]

Considering People in the Process

Another facet of the transition was highlighted in my interview with Peter Maiden. He emphasized the importance of a long transition when a founder steps aside. Within the organization, much time was given for communication and for opportunities to process. A unique feature of Operation Mobilization had been its cohesiveness based on relationships and oral traditions. When Verwer stepped aside, time had to be taken to write job descriptions and establish accountability structures. A decision was made to place a time limit on the international director position: a maximum of three terms of four years each.[16]

Maiden also recounted some of the pain in the process, which he attributed to underlying issues in the movement itself. Similar to other nonprofits, OM began as a Western movement but has become, over time, very multicultural. The non-Western staff trusted Verwer and wanted to make sure they would be represented as the leadership shifted. The issue of global representation is key and ongoing. Maiden considers it the biggest challenge in missions leadership today: "the challenge to incorporate the 'Global South,' with their styles and giftings." He elaborated further: "It costs time, money, and effort; but if we do this right, it will be our gift to Operation Mobilization. If we don't, it could be the start of decline."[17]

Besides these issues, however, Maiden described the transition as "pain free." He did reiterate that it took a long time—bringing distraction at times—since so much work had to be done to facilitate the changeover. But he noted that the next transition would be shorter, since OM would not be replacing the founder again.[18]

Generational Differences

Within the leadership transition of Operation Mobilization, one can see the evidence of diverse generations serving together. First, George Verwer came from the Silent Generation. His lifestyle captures many of the traits of that generational cohort: highly responsible, committed, God-fearing, moral, and willing to deny oneself to get the job done. Integrity and keeping one's word is paramount. A sense of vision or calling that is compelling is essential, because decisions are made that have implications for years down the road. Leaders from this era focus on getting things done, regardless of the cost. Groups like Operation Mobilization would not exist without these characteristics. Numerous ministries that have worldwide influence were founded in this same time frame (1950s and 1960s).

Verwer's successor, Peter Maiden, is an early Boomer. These folks tend to have similar character traits as those from the Silent Generation: highly responsible, committed, and willing to sacrifice. Verwer described Maiden as "a very humble, godly man who is not easily offended. More phlegmatic and diplomatic."[19]

Maiden completed his first four-year term in 2007 and is

currently in his second term, but he is definitely looking at the next generation of leadership. In fact, two hundred Gen X leaders have been selected for training in the organization. Executive leaders are setting aside time to meet with them. The leadership is looking to the future.

When I asked Maiden about the characteristics he sees in Gen Xers, he quickly listed the following:

- They are not as interested in title or position.
- Relationships are paramount.
- They expect leaders to be available.
- They desire transparent leaders who are willing to explain why and who don't just give directives.
- Leaders must earn the right to be heard.[20]

All of these points resonate with current research, both empirical and interview-based.[21]

Finally, I asked Maiden about the Millennial Generation, some of OM's newest volunteers. "Perhaps a little too early to say," he responded, "but I think they want stronger, more directive leadership again."[22] Time will tell.

Click. Photo taken. Your excursion through the pages of this book is complete. Congratulations!

You too may have screamed a few times as we navigated

the rapids of leadership succession between the generations. That's okay. The thunderous roar of the white water of your circumstances probably drowned out your cries. Your own organizational river awaits you. Perhaps it is a small business, a nonprofit, a church, a school, a clinic, a law firm, or a large corporation. It doesn't matter. Whatever your situation, the generations are real, and we're in this boat together. Transitions are coming. There *is* a way to navigate through them. Hopefully this book has equipped you to do that more successfully. Hang on to your life jacket, grab your paddle, and let's get started!

Epilogue

Are you wondering if this idea of team building via white-water rafting is too wild to believe? After experiencing white-water rafting firsthand, I have found the analogy to be the best word picture I can think of related to leadership transition. But then, just a few months before this manuscript was due, a friend sent me an article that she had torn out of the July 2007 United Airlines flight magazine. Entitled "A Buoyant Business," the article is about corporate leaders going white-water rafting so that they can work together and communicate. Amazing, eh? So I encourage you to use the principles in this book to help navigate through your own organizational transitions. Maybe you should consider a rafting trip, too!

Endnotes

Chapter One: I'll Guide the Raft

1. The expression "birth cohort" was first used in 1863 by the French sociologist Émile Littré. Generational cohorts can be traced back to Karl Mannheim's essay on the "Sociological Problem of Generations," written in 1928.

2. Tom Brokaw, *The Greatest Generation* (New York: Dell Publishing, 1998).

3. William Strauss and Neil Howe, *Generations: The History of America's Future, 1584 to 2069* (New York: William Morrow and Company, 1991); Howard Schuman and Jacqueline Scott, "Generations and Collective Memories," *American Sociological Review* 54 (1989): 359–81; Frederick D. Weil, "Cohorts, Regimes, and the Legitimation of Democracy: West Germany Since 1945," *American Sociological Review* 52 (1987): 308–24;

Ruth Cherrington, "Generational Issues in China: A Case Study of the 1980s Generation of Young Intellectuals," *British Journal of Sociology* 48, no. 2 (1997): 302–20; Cheng Li, *China's Leaders: The New Generation* (Lanham, MD: Rowman & Littlefield, 2001).

4. Cate Bower and Marybeth Fidler, "The Importance of Generational Literacy," *Association Management* 46, no. 1 (1994): 30–35; Kath Donovan and Ruth Myors, "Reflections on Attrition in Career Missionaries: A Generational Perspective into the Future," in *Too Valuable to Lose: Exploring the Causes and Cures of Missionary Attrition*, ed. William D. Taylor (Pasadena, CA: William Carey Library, 1997), 41–73; Carole L. Jurkiewicz and Roger G. Brown, "GenXers vs. Boomers vs. Matures: Generational Comparisons of Public Employee Motivation," *Review of Public Personnel Administration* 18, no. 4 (1998): 18–37; Betty R. Kupperschmidt, "Multigeneration Employees: Strategies for Effective Management," *Health Care Manager* 19, no. 1 (2000): 65–76; Ron Zemke, Claire Raines, and Bob Filipczak, "Generation Gaps in the Classroom," *Training* 36, no. 11 (1999): 48–54.

Chapter Two: Give Me the Oar

1. Gary O'Bannon, "Managing Our Future: The Generation X Factor," *Public Personnel Management* 30, no. 1 (2001): 95–109.

2. "Born of Controversy: The GI Bill of Rights," United States Department of Veteran Affairs website, http://www.gibill.va.gov/GI_Bill_Info/history.htm.

3. Betty R. Kupperschmidt, "Multigeneration Employees: Strategies for Effective Management," *Health Care Manager* 19, no. 1 (2000): 65–76; William Strauss and Neil Howe, *Generations: The History of America's Future, 1584 to 2069* (New York: William Morrow and Company, 1991); Ron Zemke, Claire Raines, and Bob Filipczak, "Generation Gaps in the Classroom," *Training* 36, no. 11 (1999): 48–54.

4. Zemke, Raines, and Filipczak, "Generation Gaps in the Classroom," 48–54.

5. Cate Bower and Marybeth Fidler, "The Importance of Generational Literacy," *Association Management* 46, no. 1 (1994): 30–35.

6. Bower and Fidler, "The Importance of Generational Literacy," 30–35; Kupperschmidt, "Multigeneration Employees," 65–76; Strauss and Howe, *Generations: The History of America's Future*; Zemke, Raines, and Filipczak, "Generation Gaps in the Classroom," 48–54.

7. Cathleen O'Connor Schoultz, "Getting the Busters and Keeping the Boomers," *Association Management* 49, no. 6 (1997): 44–49.

Chapter Three: Let's Collaborate

1. Roberta Maynard, "A Less-Stressed Work Force," *Nation's Business* 84, no. 11 (1996): 50–51; Donald E. Miller and Arpi Misha Miller, "Understanding Generation X: Values, Politics, and Religious Commitments," in *GenX Religion*, ed. Richard W. Flory and Donald E. Miller (New York: Routledge, 2000), 1–14; Shelly Reese, "The New Wave of Gen X Workers," *Business and Health* 17, no. 6 (1999): 19–23.

2. Tom Beaudoin, *Virtual Faith: The Irreverent Spiritual Quest of Generation X* (San Francisco: Jossey-Bass, 1998), 5.

3. Miller and Miller, "Understanding Generation X," 1–14.

4. Ted Halstead, "A Politics for Generation X," *The Atlantic Monthly*, August 1999, 33–42.

5. Meredith Bagby, "Celebration X," *Success* 45, no. 9 (1998): 22–23; Sally Corbo, "The X-er Files," *Hospitals and Health Networks* 71, no. 7 (1997): 58–60; Matt Dunne, "Policy Leadership, Gen X Style," *National Civic Review* 86, no. 3 (1997): 251–60; Susan M. Keaveney, "When MTV Goes CEO: What Happens When the 'Unmanageables' Become Managers?" *Marketing Management* 6, no. 3 (1997): 21–24; Randall Lane, "Computers Are Our Friends," *Forbes Magazine* 155, no. 10 (1995): 102–8; Cameron Lawrence, "Talking 'bout My Generation," *Montana Business Quarterly* 35, no. 2 (1997): 12–14; Richard Miniter, "Generation X Does Business," *American Enterprise* 8, no. 4 (1997): 38–40; Bruce Tulgan, "Generation X: Slackers? Or the Workforce of the Future?" *Employment Relations Today* 24, no. 2 (1997): 55–64.

6. Susan Ainsworth, "1996 Employment Outlook: Generation X Infiltrates Management, Breathes New Life into Corporations," *Chemical & Engineering*

News 73, no. 43 (1995): 42–50; Sally Corbo, "The X-er Files," *Hospitals and Health Networks* 71, no. 7 (1997): 58–60; Bettina A. Lankard, "Career Development in Generation X: Myths and Realities," Center on Education and Training for Employment, Ohio State University, Columbus, OH, 1995, available at Education Resources Information Center website, www.eric.ed.gov; Lane, "Computers Are Our Friends," 102–8; Bruce Tulgan, *Managing Generation X: How to Bring Out the Best in Young Talent* (Oxford: Capstone, 1996).

7. Miller and Miller, "Understanding Generation X," 1–14.

8. Halstead, "A Politics for Generation X," 33–42.

9. Maynard, "A Less-Stressed Work Force," 50–51; Reese, "The New Wave of Gen X Workers," 19–23.

Chapter Four: Whatever

1. Neil Howe and William Strauss, *Millennials Rising: The Next Great Generation* (New York: Vintage Books, 2000), 14–15; Judy Denny, review of *Millennials Rising: The Next Great Generation*, by Neil Howe and William Strauss, The Federal Consulting Group, U.S. Department of the Treasury, October 2004, http://www.fcg.gov/documents/Millennials_Rising_bkreview.pdf, 1.

2. Madsen Pirie and Robert M. Worcester, *The Millennial Generation* (London: Adam Smith Institute, 1998); Denny, review of *Millennials Rising*, 1–2.

3. Claire Raines, "Managing Millennials," http://www.generationsatwork.com/articles/millenials.htm, excerpted from *Connecting Generations: The Sourcebook for a New Workplace* (Menlo Park, CA: Crisp Publications, 2003).

4. Howe and Strauss, *Millennials Rising;* Mark L. Taylor, "Generation NeXt Comes to College: 2006 Updates and Emerging Issues," in *A Collection of Papers on Self-Study and Institutional Improvement* (Chicago: The Higher Learning Commission, 2006), 48.

5. Taylor, "Generation NeXt Comes to College," 48.

6. Raines, "Managing Millennials"; Howe and Strauss, *Millennials Rising.*

7. Mischa Gaus, "Hey Millennials, Debt Becomes You," *In These Times*, May 18, 2006, http://www.inthesetimes.com/article/2619.

8. Pirie and Worcester, *The Millennial Generation*, 8; Gaus, "Hey Millennials, Debt Becomes You."

9. Mel Levine, "College Graduates Aren't Ready for the Real World," *The Chronicle of Higher Education* 51, no. 24 (February 2005), http://chronicle.com/free/v51/i24/24b01101.htm.

10. Pirie and Worcester, *The Millennial Generation*, 8; Melissa H. Sandfort and Jennifer G. Haworth, "Whassup? A Glimpse into the Attitudes and Beliefs of the Millennial Generation," *Journal of College and Character*, no. 2 (2005), http://www.collegevalues.org/articles.cfm?id=613&a=1.

11. Don Tapscott, *Growing Up Digital: The Rise of the Net Generation* (New York: McGraw-Hill, 2006).

12. Raines, "Managing Millennials"; W. S. Smith, "Employers and the New Generation of Employees," *Community College Journal*, December 2005/ January 2006, 8–13.

Chapter Six: Big Mama

1. Camille Bishop, "Generational Cohorts and Cultural Diversity as Factors Affecting Leadership Transition in Organizations" (PhD diss, Trinity International University, 2004), 93; Warren G. Bennis and Robert J. Thomas, *Geeks and Geezers* (Cambridge, MA: Harvard Business School Press, 2002), 47–49.

2. Valerie I. Sessa, Robert J. Kabacoff, Jennifer Deal, and Heather Brown, "Generational Differences in Leader Values and Leadership Behaviors," *The Psychologist-Manager Journal* 10, no. 1 (2007): 47–74.

3. Bishop, "Generational Cohorts and Cultural Diversity," 76.

4. Cate Bower and Marybeth Fidler, "The Importance of Generational Literacy," *Association Management* 46, no. 1 (1994): 30–35; Kath Donovan and Ruth Myors, "Reflections on Attrition in Career Missionaries: A Generational Perspective into the Future," in *Too Valuable to Lose: Exploring the Causes and Cures of Missionary Attrition*, ed. William D. Taylor (Pasadena,

CA: William Carey Library, 1997), 41–73; Carole L. Jurkiewicz and Roger G. Brown, "GenXers vs. Boomers vs. Matures: Generational Comparisons of Public Employee Motivation," *Review of Public Personnel Administration* 18, no. 4 (1998): 18–37; Betty R. Kupperschmidt, "Multigeneration Employees: Strategies for Effective Management," *Health Care Manager* 19, no. 1 (2000): 65–76; William Strauss and Neil Howe, *Generations: The History of America's Future, 1584 to 2069* (New York: William Morrow and Company, 1991); Ron Zemke, Claire Raines, and Bob Filipczak, "Generation Gaps in the Classroom," *Training* 36, no. 11 (1999): 48–54; Ron Zemke, Claire Raines, and Bob Filipczak, *Generations at Work: Managing the Clash of Veterans, Boomers, Xers, and Nexters in Your Workplace* (New York: AMACOM, 2000), 63–91.

5. Bishop, "Generational Cohorts and Cultural Diversity," 79.

6. Bishop, "Generational Cohorts and Cultural Diversity," 79; Sessa, Kabacoff, Deal, and Brown, "Generational Differences in Leader Values," 47–74.

7. Bishop, "Generational Cohorts and Cultural Diversity," 80.

8. Sessa, Kabacoff, Deal, and Brown, "Generational Differences in Leader Values," 47–74.

9. Bishop, "Generational Cohorts and Cultural Diversity," 139–40.

Chapter Seven: Disaster Falls

1. Daniel Goleman, "Leadership That Gets Results," *Harvard Business Review* 78, no. 2 (2000): 78–90.

2. Camille Bishop, "Generational Cohorts and Cultural Diversity as Factors Affecting Leadership Transition in Organizations" (PhD diss, Trinity International University, 2004), 93.

3. Bishop, "Generational Cohorts and Cultural Diversity," 93; Valerie I. Sessa, Robert J. Kabacoff, Jennifer Deal, and Heather Brown, "Generational Differences in Leader Values and Leadership Behaviors," *The Psychologist-Manager Journal* 10, no. 1 (2007): 47–74.

4. Bishop, "Generational Cohorts and Cultural Diversity," 93.

5. Sessa, Kabacoff, Deal, and Brown, "Generational Differences in Leader Values," 47–74.

6. Bishop, "Generational Cohorts and Cultural Diversity," 99.

7. Ibid., 100–103.

8. Nadira A. Hira, "Attracting the Twentysomething Worker," *Fortune*, May 15, 2007, http://money.cnn.com/magazines/fortune/fortune_archive/2007/05/28/100033934/index.htm.

Chapter Eight: Lost Paddle

1. Camille Bishop, "Generational Cohorts and Cultural Diversity as Factors Affecting Leadership Transition in Organizations" (PhD diss, Trinity International University, 2004), 94.

2. Ibid., 106.

3. Ibid., 105.

4. Ibid., 108.

5. Ibid., 94–96.

6. Ibid., 204.

7. Ibid., 19–20.

8. Focus group led by author, Hong Kong, March 21, 2007. The focus group was comprised of approximately fifteen university students who were all Millennials and came from diverse cultures (UK, USA, South Africa, Hong Kong, Philippines, Holland, Denmark, Canada).

Chapter Nine: Bus Stop

1. Camille Bishop, "Generational Cohorts and Cultural Diversity as Factors Affecting Leadership Transition in Organizations" (PhD diss, Trinity International University, 2004), 85.

2. Ibid.

3. Ibid.

4. Ibid.

5. Ibid., 86.

6. Ibid., 86–87.

7. Ibid., 87–88.

8. Ibid., 88.

9. Ibid., 89.

10. Nadira A. Hira, "Attracting the Twentysomething Worker," *Fortune*, May 15, 2007, http://money.cnn.com/magazines/fortune/fortune_archive/2007/05/28/100033934/index.htm.

Chapter Ten: Table Saw

1. John Maxwell, *The 21 Indispensable Qualities of a Leader* (Nashville: Thomas Nelson, 1998), IX.

2. Jane Kennard, "Literature from the Social Sciences That Informs Approaches to Leadership in the Church" (unpublished paper, Trinity Evangelical Divinity School, 1998), 6.

3. Edwin P. Hollander and Lynn R. Offermann, "Power and Leadership in Organizations," *The American Psychologist* 45, no. 2 (1990): 179–87.

4. Kennard, "Literature from the Social Sciences," 26–27.

5. Peter Drucker, quoted in John Borek, Danny Lovett, and Elmer Towns, *The Good Book on Leadership: Case Studies from the Bible* (Nashville: Broadman & Holman, 2005), 70.

6. Bernard M. Bass, "From Transactional to Transformational Leadership: Learning to Share the Vision," *Organizational Dynamics* 18, no. 3 (1990): 19–20.

7. Warren Bennis, *On Becoming a Leader* (Reading, MA: Addison-Wesley, 1989); Peter F. Drucker, *Managing the Nonprofit Organization* (New York: Harper Collins, 1990); Hollander and Offermann, "Power and Leadership in Organizations," 179–87; Robert Stanley Paul, "Growing Leaders: The Art of Nurturing Leaders for Christian Ministry" (DMin project, Fuller Theological Seminary, 1990).

8. Daniel Goleman, Richard Boyatzis, and Annie McKee, *Primal Leadership: Learning to Lead with Emotional Intelligence* (Cambridge, MA: Harvard Business School Press, 2000), 3–18.

9. Camille Bishop, "Generational Cohorts and Cultural Diversity as Factors Affecting Leadership Transition in Organizations" (PhD diss, Trinity International University, 2004), 90.

10. Ibid.

11. Valerie I. Sessa, Robert J. Kabacoff, Jennifer Deal, and Heather Brown, "Generational Differences in Leader Values and Leadership Behaviors," *The Psychologist-Manager Journal* 10, no. 1 (2007): 59.

12. Ibid.

13. Bishop, "Generational Cohorts and Cultural Diversity," 91.

14. Ibid.

15. Ibid., 92.

16. Sessa, Kabacoff, Deal, and Brown, "Generational Differences in Leader Values," 60.

17. Ibid., 59.

18. Focus group led by author, Hong Kong, March 21, 2007. The focus group was comprised of approximately fifteen university students who were all Millennials and came from diverse cultures (UK, USA, South Africa, Hong Kong, Philippines, Holland, Denmark, Canada).

Chapter Eleven: Handing Over the Rudder

1. Craig E. Aronoff, Stephen L. McClure, and John L. Ward, *Family Business Succession: The Final Test of Greatness* (Marietta, GA: Family Enterprise Publishers, 2003), 1.

2. Ibid., 1–2.

3. Bobby Clinton and Kathrine Haubert, *The Joshua Portrait: A Study in Leadership Development, Leadership Transition, and Destiny Fulfillment* (Altadena, CA: Barnabas Publishers, 1990); John Morris Dixon, "Planning for Firm Succession," *Architectural Record* 186, no. 12 (1998): 60–65;

Kevin E. Drumm, "Difficulties in Leadership Transition: A Case Study of a Community College Presidency" (PhD diss, New York University, 1995); Kevin Dyer, "Leadership Transition: Painful but Necessary," *Evangelical Missions Quarterly* 25, no. 2 (1989): 172–73; Thomas North Gilmore, *Making a Leadership Change: How Organizations and Leaders Can Handle Leadership Transitions* (San Francisco: Jossey-Bass, 1988); Thomas N. Gilmore and Robert A. Brown, "Effective Leadership Succession as a Critical Event in Social Agencies," *Administration in Social Work* 9, no. 4 (1986): 25–35; Eric Hanson and Bruce Court, "Bridging the Leadership Gap," *Performance Improvement* 37, no. 1 (1998): 8–14.

4. Aronoff, McClure, and Ward, *Family Business Succession;* Sheila Albert, *Seven Steps to an Effective Leadership Transition* (Washington, DC: National Center for Nonprofit Boards, 1996); Christine A. Culbert, "Successful Transition of Leadership in a Small Family Business" (MA thesis, College of St. Scholastica, 1998).

5. Aronoff, McClure, and Ward, *Family Business Succession*, 1.

6. Ibid.

7. Peter F. Drucker, *Managing the Nonprofit Organization* (New York: Harper Collins, 1990), 117.

8. Edgar H. Schein, "The Role of the Founder in Creating Organizational Culture," *Organizational Dynamics* 12, no. 1 (1983): 13–28.

9. Aronoff, McClure, and Ward, *Family Business Succession*, 13–19.

10. Camille Bishop, "Generational Cohorts and Cultural Diversity as Factors Affecting Leadership Transition in Organizations" (PhD diss, Trinity International University, 2004), 135.

11. Bishop, "Generational Cohorts and Cultural Diversity," 139.

12. Ibid.

13. Ibid., 140–41.

14. Ibid., 141.

15. Ibid., 138.

Chapter Twelve: Tossed Out of the Boat

1. William Bridges, *Getting Them Through the Wilderness: A Leader's Guide to Transition* (Mill Valley, CA: William Bridges & Associates, 1994), 2.

2. Diane C. Decker and James A. Belohav, "Managing Transitions," *Quality Progress* 30 (April 1997): 93–97.

3. Susan J. Ashford, "Individual Strategies for Coping with Stress during Organizational Transitions," *Journal of Applied Behavioral Science* 24, no. 1 (1988): 19–36; Michael J. Austin and Thomas N. Gilmore, "Executive Exit: Multiple Perspectives on Managing the Leadership Transition," *Administration in Social Work* 17, no. 1 (1993): 47–60; Nancy J. Barger and Linda K. Kirby, *The Challenge of Change in Organizations: Helping Employees Thrive in the New Frontier* (Palo Alto, CA: Davies-Black Publishing, 1995); John Iacovini, "The Human Side of Organization Change," *Training and Development* 47, no. 1 (1993): 65–68; Jacquelyn Phifer, "Key Leadership Behaviors Related to Affective Commitment during Organizational Transition" (MA thesis, College of St. Scholastica, 1998).

4. Charlotte Greeson, Mary Hollingsworth, and Michael Washburn, *The Grief Adjustment Guide* (Sisters, OR: Questar Publishers, 1990).

5. Patrick Lencioni, *The Five Dysfunctions of a Team: A Leadership Fable* (San Francisco: Jossey-Bass, 2002), 188.

6. Roger W. Sapp, "Honoring the Truth-teller," June 14, 2000, http://www.cyberscripture.com/htt.htm.

Chapter Fourteen: Staying in the Raft

1. Craig E. Aronoff, Stephen L. McClure, and John L. Ward, *Family Business Succession: The Final Test of Greatness* (Marietta, GA: Family Enterprise Publishers, 2003), 1.

2. Peter F. Drucker, *Managing in the Next Society* (New York: St. Martin's Press, 2002), 236–42.

3. Ibid., 236.

4. Thomas L. Friedman, *The World Is Flat: A Brief History of the Twenty-first Century* (New York: Farrar, Straus, and Giroux, 2005).

5. Drucker, *Managing in the Next Society*, 235.

6. Friedman, *The World Is Flat*, 175.

7. Drucker, *Managing in the Next Society*, 86–87.

8. Frances Hesselbein, *Hesselbein on Leadership* (San Francisco: Jossey-Bass, 2002), 41–42.

9. John Morris Dixon, "Planning for Firm Succession," *Architectural Record* 186, no. 12 (1998): 60–65; Kevin E. Drumm, "Difficulties in Leadership Transition: A Case Study of a Community College Presidency" (PhD diss, New York University, 1995); Kevin Dyer, "Leadership Transition: Painful but Necessary," *Evangelical Missions Quarterly* 25, no. 2 (1989): 172–73; Thomas N. Gilmore and Robert A. Brown, "Effective Leadership Transition as a Critical Event in Social Agencies," *Administration in Social Work* 9, no. 4 (1986): 25–35.

10. Andrew N. Garman and Jeremy Glawe, "Succession Planning," *Consulting Psychology Journal: Practice and Research* 56, no. 2 (2004): 119–28.

11. Sheila Albert, *Seven Steps to an Effective Leadership Transition* (Washington, DC: National Center for Nonprofit Boards, 1996); Christine A. Culbert, "Successful Transition of Leadership in a Small Family Business" (MA thesis, College of St. Scholastica, 1998).

12. Jeff Wuorio, "The Succession Crisis: Nearly Half of All Family Businesses Will Change Hands in the Near Future. Is Yours Prepared? (Most Don't Have a Clue)," *Success* (1998): 76–81.

13. Frank Stasiowski, "How to Plan for the Inevitable," *Engineering News-Record*, July 2005 Sourcebook, vol. 254, issue 25A: 103.

14. Jack Welch, *Jack: Straight from the Gut* (New York: Warner Books, 2001), 407–8.

15. Jack Welch, *Winning* (New York: Harper Collins, 2005), 41–42.

16. Peter F. Drucker, *Managing the Nonprofit Organization* (New York: Harper Collins, 1990), 117.

17. Betsy Morris, "No. 1 Genentech: The Best Place to Work Now," *Fortune*, January 31, 2006, http://money.cnn.com/magazines/fortune/fortune_archive/2006/01/23/8366989/index.htm.

18. Ron Zemke, Claire Raines, and Bob Filipczak, *Generations at Work: Managing the Clash of Veterans, Boomers, Xers, and Nexters in Your Workplace* (New York: AMACOM, 2000), 159.

Chapter Fifteen: Handing Over the Oar

1. Robert Slater, *Jack Welch and the GE Way: Management Insights and Leadership Secrets of the Legendary CEO* (New York: McGraw-Hill, 1999), 19–20.

2. Jeffrey A. Krames, *What the Best CEOs Know: Seven Exceptional Leaders and Their Lessons for Transforming Any Business* (New York: McGraw-Hill, 2003), 10.

3. Slater, *Jack Welch and the GE Way*, 64–65.

4. See General Electric's website, www.ge.com.

5. Robert Slater, *The Wal-Mart Decade* (New York: Portfolio, 2003), 32–35.

6. Ibid., 71–74.

7. Ibid., 87.

8. Ibid., 48–53.

9. Ibid., 87.

10. Louis V. Gerstner Jr., *Who Says Elephants Can't Dance? Inside IBM's Historic Turnaround* (New York: Harper Business, 2002), 30.

11. John Pierce, "Habitat Founder and Board Disagree on His Retirement Date," *Christian Century*, October 5, 2004: 15.

12. "These Days, Too Few Heed the Call," *The Economist*, June 28, 2001.

13. Ibid.

Chapter Sixteen: Finishing the Course

1. "The History of OM," Operation Mobilization website, http://www.om.org/history.html.

2. Ibid.

3. George Verwer, phone interview with author, December 8, 2006.

4. Ibid.

5. Ibid.

6. Ibid.

7. Peter Maiden, phone interview with author, March 28, 2007.

8. "Who Is Peter Maiden?" Operation Mobilization website, http://www.om.org/about/who-is-peter-maiden.html.

9. Maiden interview.

10. Verwer interview.

11. Ibid.

12. Ibid.

13. Maiden interview.

14. Verwer interview.

15. Ibid.

16. Maiden interview.

17. Ibid.

18. Ibid.

19. Verwer interview.

20. Maiden interview.

21. Camille Bishop, "Generational Cohorts and Cultural Diversity as Factors Affecting Leadership Transition in Organizations" (PhD diss, Trinity International University, 2004); Valerie I. Sessa, Robert J. Kabacoff, Jennifer Deal, and Heather Brown, "Generational Differences in Leader Values and

Leadership Behaviors," *The Psychologist-Manager Journal* 10, no. 1 (2007): 47–74.

22. Maiden interview.